Klaus W. Jonas
William Somerset Maugham

Klaus W. Jonas

William Somerset Maugham
The Man and His Work / Leben und Werk

2009
Harrassowitz Verlag · Wiesbaden

Bibliografische Information der Deutschen Nationalbibliothek
Die Deutsche Nationalbibliothek verzeichnet diese Publikation in der Deutschen
Nationalbibliografie; detaillierte bibliografische Daten sind im Internet
über http://dnb.d-nb.de abrufbar.

Bibliographic information published by the Deutsche Nationalbibliothek
The Deutsche Nationalbibliothek lists this publication in the Deutsche
Nationalbibliografie; detailed bibliographic data are available in the internet
at http://dnb.d-nb.de.

Informationen zum Verlagsprogramm finden Sie unter
http://www.harrassowitz-verlag.de
© Otto Harrassowitz GmbH & Co. KG, Wiesbaden 2009
Kreuzberger Ring 7c-d, D-65205 Wiesbaden,
produktsicherheit.verlag@harrassowitz.de
Das Werk einschließlich aller seiner Teile ist urheberrechtlich geschützt.
Jede Verwertung außerhalb der engen Grenzen des Urheberrechtsgesetzes ist ohne
Zustimmung des Verlages unzulässig und strafbar. Das gilt insbesondere
für Vervielfältigungen jeder Art, Übersetzungen, Mikroverfilmungen und
für die Einspeicherung in elektronische Systeme.
Druck und Verarbeitung: BoD, Hamburg
Printed in Germany
ISBN 978-3-447-06142-1
e-ISBN PDF 978-3-447-19202-6

*Für
Ilsedore*

Contents – Inhalt

Preface	IX
(Vorwort)	XI
Author's Preface	1
(Zu dieser Edition)	3
Chronicle of Maugham's Life	7
(Leben Somerset Maughams)	17
The Maugham Enigma	29
Der Gentleman von Cap Ferrat	39
Aus dem Briefwechsel mit Somerset Maugham	55
Bibliography of Maugham's Own Literary Work	77
(Somerset Maughams Werk)	
Bibliography of Secondary Literature	83
(Literatur über Somerset Maugham)	
Index of Personal Names	125
(Personenregister)	
Index of Places	127
(Ortsregister)	
Index of Works	129
(Werkregister)	
Abbildungen	133

Preface

W. Somerset Maugham

Villa Mauresque
St. Jean, Cap Ferrat, A.M.
14th May, 1956

Dear Klaus,

It is a difficult job you have given me. I do not know whether you wish to place this piece you ask me to write as a preface to what you have written or as a postscript. I have a great dislike to reading anything that is concerned with myself or my works. Several books have been written about me; I have not read them. When first I had books published, I subscribed to a press agency, but when the first World War broke out it happened that I was here and there, and out of reach, and afterwards I took long journeys to distant countries. The result was that often I did not get my press cuttings for several weeks, and sometimes for months, after they had appeared. They came then in a large packet and I found them of no great interest. I ceased to subscribe to the agency and since then I have never read a review of anything I have written except when by chance I happened to find one in the newspaper I was reading. The advantage of that is that when I am told that an old friend of mine has violently attacked me in some paper I can greet him, when I run across him, with my usual cordiality. The fact is that when I have written something, corrected the proof and published it, I am no longer interested in it and don't really care what people say about it.

I have never pretended to be anything but a story writer. I have little patience with the novelists who preach or philosophise. I think it much better to leave philosophy to the philosophers and social reform to the social reformer. It has amused me to write stories, plays and novels. With the exception of the last war, when I was called upon to write propaganda, a thing for which I had no gift and so found a distressing burden, I have only written for my own pleasure. Do not suppose I mean by this that I have found it easy to write. Over and over again I have spent a whole day writing and rewriting a single page and in the end left it, not because I was satisfied with it, but because I could do no better. So far as I know, there are but two ways of writing English, the plain and the ornate. When I began to write, the ornate was in vogue and, as was natural in a very young man, I sought to follow it. I had no bent for it. After wasting a good deal of time, I came to the conclusion that it suited me better to eschew the flowery, the precious, the artificial, and to write as simply and naturally as I could, to write as far as possible as I would talk. I should like to think that I have not entirely failed. The most pleasing compliment I have ever received came from a G.I. in the last war who was stationed in New Guinea; he wrote to tell me that he had greatly enjoyed a book of mine that he had been reading because he had never had to look out a single word in the dictionary.

During the sixty years I have been writing, I have written a great deal. I have written over a hundred stories, between twenty and thirty plays and between twenty and thirty novels. It has been borne in upon me that a good many people are angry with me because my various works have brought me in a great deal of money. That is silly. They ought rather to be angry with the people all over the world who buy my books and pay to go to see my plays. I have written because I had a fertile invention and the ideas for plays and stories that thronged my brain would not let me rest till I had got rid of them by writing them. But that is a thing of the past. With age one's inventiveness leaves one and it is long since I have been troubled with any subject that insisted on being turned into a piece of fiction.

But I like writing. For well over half a century I have been in the habit of shutting myself up in a room every morning and writing till lunch time. Do you know the story of the elderly Frenchman who had been accustomed for twenty years to spend every evening with his mistress? One day a friend asked him: „But after all these years why on earth don't you marry her?" His face fell. „Where then should I spend my evenings?" he answered. I am like the elderly Frenchman; if I didn't write, how should I pass my mornings? I am well aware that I have lost any talent I may have had. There was only one thing for me to do – to turn critic.

Yours sincerely,
W.S. Maugham

Vorwort

W. Somerset Maugham

Villa Mauresque
St. Jean, Cap Ferrat, A.M.
14. Mai 1956

Lieber Klaus,
Es ist eine schwierige Aufgabe, die Du mir gestellt hast. Ich weiß nicht, ob Du diesen Brief, um den Du mich gebeten hast, als Vor- oder Nachwort zu Deinem eigenen Text benutzen willst. Ich habe eine starke Abneigung dagegen, irgend etwas über mich selbst oder mein Werk zu lesen. Mehrere Bücher sind über mich geschrieben worden; ich habe sie nicht gelesen. Als ich zum ersten Mal als Schriftsteller hervortrat, hatte ich ein Abonnement bei einem Zeitungsausschnittbüro, doch als der Erste Weltkrieg ausbrach, war ich viel unterwegs und nur schwer zu erreichen. Und später unternahm ich ausgedehnte Reisen in ferne Länder. Daher vergingen oft Wochen, bisweilen Monate, ehe ich die in der Zwischenzeit in der Tagespresse erschienenen Artikel zu sehen bekam. Schließlich erreichten sie mich in einem großen Paket und ich fand sie einfach nicht besonders interessant. So kam ich dann zu dem Entschluß, meine Subskription bei der Agentur aufzugeben, und seitdem lese ich keine Rezensionen mehr über meine Arbeiten, es sei denn, ich finde durch Zufall eine Besprechung in der jeweiligen Zeitung, die ich gerade lese. Der Vorteil liegt darin, dass – wenn man mir sagt, ein alter Freund habe mich in irgend einer Zeitung heftig angegriffen – ich diesen bei einer zufälligen Begegnung mit gewohnter Herzlichkeit begrüßen kann. Es ist also wirklich so, dass – wenn ich einmal etwas zu Papier gebracht, die Druckfahnen berichtigt und das Ganze veröffentlicht habe – ich nicht mehr daran interessiert bin und es mir ganz und gar gleichgültig ist, was die Leute darüber sagen.

Ich habe niemals den Anspruch erhoben, mehr als ein Erzähler zu sein. Ich habe wenig Geduld mit Romanschriftstellern, die predigen oder philosophieren. Mir scheint es viel richtiger, das Philosophieren den Philosophen zu überlassen und die Sozialreformen den Sozialreformern. Es hat mir Freude gemacht, Erzählungen, Dramen und Romane zu schreiben. Mit Ausnahme des letzten Krieges, in dem ich zu Propagandazwecken schreiben mußte – übrigens eine Tätigkeit, für die ich keinerlei Begabung hatte und die ich folglich als unangenehme Last empfand – habe ich nur zu meinem eigenen Vergnügen geschrieben. Man solle nun aber ja nicht glauben, ich hätte das Schreiben als leicht empfunden. Immer wieder habe ich einen ganzen Tag damit verbracht, eine einzige Seite zu schreiben und noch einmal zu schreiben, und am Ende habe ich es aufgegeben, nicht weil ich mit dem Resultat wirklich zufrieden war, sondern weil ich es einfach nicht besser konnte. Soweit ich weiß, gibt es nur zwei Wege, Englisch zu schreiben: den einfachen und den preziösen. Der letztere war populär, als ich meine Laufbahn als Schriftsteller begann, und wie es bei einem sehr jungen Mann nur natürlich war, suchte ich diesen Weg einzuschlagen. Aber ich hatte gar keine Neigung dafür. Nachdem ich also viel Zeit vergeudet hatte, kam ich zu der Erkenntnis, dass es für mich viel besser wäre, eine solch preziöse Sprache zu vermeiden und stattdessen so einfach zu schreiben, wie ich es nur konnte, mit anderen Worten: so weit wie möglich die gesprochene Umgangssprache zu benutzen. Ich kann wohl behaupten, in diesem Bemühen nicht völlig versagt zu haben. Das erfreulichste Kompliment, das ich je bekommen habe, kam im letzten Krieg von einem auf Neuguinea stationierten amerikanischen GI, der mir schrieb, er habe eins meiner Bücher zum Teil darum so sehr genossen, weil er kein einziges Wort hätte im Lexikon nachschlagen müssen.

Während der letzten sechzig Jahre, in denen ich als Schriftsteller hervorgetreten bin, habe ich sehr viel geschrieben: mehr als hundert Erzählungen, zwischen zwanzig und dreißig Theaterstücke und zwischen zwanzig und dreißig Romane. Man hat mich wissen lassen, dass viele Leute sich über mich ärgern, weil meine Werke mir sehr viel Geld einbringen. Dies Argument halte ich für töricht. Die Leute sollten sich lieber über all die Menschen in der Welt ärgern, die meine Bücher kaufen und die Geld bezahlen, um meine Theaterstücke zu sehen. Ich habe meine Werke geschrieben, weil ich eine lebhafte Phantasie besitze und die Ideen für meine Stücke und Erzählungen, die ich im Kopf hatte, mir einfach keine Ruhe ließen, bis ich sie niedergeschrieben hatte. Aber das alles ist nun Teil der Vergangenheit. Mit zunehmendem Alter nimmt die Erfindungsgabe ab und es ist schon lange her, seit irgend ein Thema mich derart intensiv beschäftigt hat, dass ich es unbedingt in ein Theaterstück oder eine Erzählung hätte verwandeln müssen.

Aber das Schreiben macht mir noch immer Spaß. Seit mehr als einem halben Jahrhundert ist es meine Routine, mich jeden Morgen in mein Zimmer einzuschließen und bis zum Mittagessen zu schreiben. Sag mal, kennst

Du eigentlich die Geschichte von dem alten Franzosen, der zwanzig Jahre lang die Gewohnheit hatte, jeden Abend bei seiner Geliebten zu verbringen? Eines Tages fragte ihn ein Freund: „Aber warum hast Du sie nach all diesen Jahren denn nicht geheiratet?" Er machte ein verdutztes Gesicht: „Wo sollte ich dann meine Abende verbringen?", gab er zur Antwort. Mir geht es ähnlich wie dem alten Franzosen: Wenn ich nicht schreiben könnte, wie sollte ich dann meine Morgenstunden verbringen? Es ist mir durchaus klar, dass ich jedwedes Talent, das ich in früheren Jahren besessen, verloren habe. Und so gab es dann nur noch eins für mich – Kritiker zu werden.

Stets Dein
W.S. Maugham

Author's Preface

For a number of years the fiction of W. Somerset Maugham has been enjoying a veritable renaissance, especially in the German-speaking countries. He is undoubtedly considered the most widely-read English author of the first half of the twentieth century. Unquestionably, his Swiss publisher, Diogenes Verlag in Zurich, deserves credit for its wise decision to reissue all of Maugham's novels and short stories in new translations. The first volume in this series was a German edition of *A Writer's Notebook* (*Notizbuch eines Schriftstellers*, 2004), edited by Simone and Thomas Stölzel with an eighty-page introduction to the stupendous life-work of this „teller of tales", as Maugham liked to call himself.

In the last decade of his long life, Maugham repeatedly stressed that he would never read anything about himself or his work. In fact, he asked his friends throughout the world to destroy his letters, and in his Last Will and Testament, he urged them never to give any aid to would-be biographers.

In spite of his basic aversion to critics who, he felt, had often done him an injustice, and his strong dislike of biographical projects about him of any kind, there have been a few exceptions to this rule.

Three scholars have had the good fortune to benefit from his complete confidence. These critics, he felt, were entitled to his full support: A Frenchman, an American and a German-born bibliographer and collector whose publications on Maugham have made their appearance both on the American and European Continent.

As early as the late nineteen twenties, Paul Dottin, a professor of English and later President of the University of Toulouse, published the first of two major monographs dealing with Maugham's plays and his fiction. He was permitted to send long questionnaires to the author and received more than thirty hand-written answers. In 1966, Dottin donated his complete collection of research materials to the Center of Maugham Studies. After Maugham's death, they were turned over to the Humanities Research Center of the University of Texas in Austin, renowned for one of the most comprehensive Maugham collections in existence.

Since 1937, Richard A. Cordell of Purdue University, a well-known critic of the *Saturday Review of Literature*, published a number of biographical and critical studies of Maugham's life and work. Maugham wholeheartedly approved of these efforts, and their author became a member of a small inner circle of close personal friends always welcome at the Villa Mauresque

In the German-speaking countries, a good many academic studies, mostly doctoral dissertations, have appeared since the mid-thirties. The only important scholarly study, however, was written by Helmut Papajewski of Berlin University, published in 1952 by the Cologne University Press. After reading the first chapter, Maugham was deeply impressed and even planned to interest his English publisher, Alexander S. Frere of William Heinemann in London, in having it translated. Later, however, Maugham was disappointed and soon gave up any such plans. To this day it has not been published outside of Germany.

In contrast to the above-mentioned publications, our own contributions appeared both in German and in English and, occasionally, in Japanese (e.g. *The World of Somerset Maugham*, translated by Mutsuo Tanaka). Inasmuch as these volumes and essays have long been out of print, we have decided to publish this book. It contains Maugham's preface written as an introduction to the volume *The Gentleman from Cap Ferrat* (1956), as well as two lectures. One of them was given in English in 1966 at the University of Pittsburgh, the other in German in 1972 at a symposium of Pittsburgh University and Carnegie-Mellon professors and later published in the volume *Universitätstage in Biberach*, edited by Heinz Sauereßig.

Our personal reminiscences were written especially for the present volume and include excerpts from my twenty-year correspondence with Somerset Maugham and Alan Searle. A select bibliography both of Maugham's own writings and critical studies in English, French, German and Japanese conclude this volume.

I am grateful to Thomas Breitenauer (Technische Universität München) for preparing the layout and for the close collaboration during the past year. My special thanks to Julia Guthmüller of Harrassowitz Verlag for her encouragement, her advice and helpful suggestions.

My sincere appreciation goes to Thomas F. Staley, a University of Pittsburgh colleague about fifty years ago and long-time Director of the Harry Ransom Humanities Research Center of the University of Texas in Austin for his kindness and assistance in the preparation of this volume.

Klaus W. Jonas, Munich, Summer 2009

Zu dieser Edition

Seit mehreren Jahren erlebt das erzählerische Werk William Somerset Maughams, des meistgelesenen englischen Schriftstellers der ersten Hälfte des 20. Jahrhunderts, eine wahre Renaissance. Wesentlichen Anteil daran hat zweifellos der Diogenes Verlag Zürich, der sich entschlossen hat, sämtliche Erzählungen und Romane dieses „homme de lettres" in neuen Übersetzungen herauszubringen. Als erster Band in dieser Reihe erschien im Jahre 2004 das *Notizbuch eines Schriftstellers* (*A Writer's Notebook*) mit einem achtzigseitigen Essay der beiden Herausgeber, Simone und Thomas Stölzel, über den „Menschenkenner und Gentleman-Autor", eine erste Einführung in das kaum noch überschaubare Lebenswerk dieses „Teller of Tales", wie er sich selbst gern bezeichnete.

In den letzten Jahrzehnten seines Lebens hat Maugham wiederholt betont, dass er niemals etwas über sich und sein Werk lesen würde. Sowohl durch die Medien als auch in seinem Testament hat er Freunde und Briefpartner gebeten, etwaige Arbeiten an einer Biographie in keiner Weise zu unterstützen und seine Briefe zu vernichten. Vergeblich hatte sein Sekretär Alan Searle versucht, zu retten, was noch zu retten war, doch das Gros seiner persönlichen Dokumente hat er einige Jahre vor seinem Lebensende selbst den Flammen übergeben.

Trotz Maughams grundsätzlicher Abneigung gegen Kritiker, mit denen er oft schlechte Erfahrungen gemacht hat, vor allem aber gegen biographische Projekte über ihn, gab es einige wenige Ausnahmen. Drei Literaturwissenschaftler, ein Franzose, ein gebürtiger Amerikaner und ein auf beiden Kontinenten aktiver Amerika-Deutscher hatten das Glück, seine Wertschätzung und sein vollkommenes Vertrauen zu genießen. Jeden von ihnen hat er bei ihren Bemühungen um objektive Beurteilung seiner Lebensleistung als Mensch und als Schriftsteller in jeder Weise unterstützt.

Bereits in den späten zwanziger Jahren hat sich der französische Anglist Paul Dottin eingehend mit seinem Werk beschäftigt und zwei Monographien vorgelegt, denen Maughams sorgfältige Antworten auf seine diversen Fragebögen wesentlich zugute kamen. Etwa dreißig Briefe von Maughams Hand hat Dottin im Laufe der Jahre erhalten und dem von uns begründeten „Center of Maugham Studies" gestiftet. Seit 1966 werden sie im Humanities Research Center der University of Texas, einer der größten Maugham-Sammlungen auf der Welt, aufbewahrt.

Seit 1937 erschienen verschiedene Monographien und Editionen des amerikanischen Literaturwissenschaftlers Richard A. Cordell. Seine Interpretationen sowie die biographischen Informationen fanden Maughams volle Unterstützung. Während Dottins Arbeiten ausschließlich in Frankreich erschienen und nie – von einer Ausnahme abgesehen – ins Englische übersetzt wurden, waren Cordells Studien nur in Großbritannien, Kanada und den Vereinigten Staaten in seiner Muttersprache erschienen.

Im deutschen Sprachgebiet erschienen im Laufe der Jahre zwar verschiedene Dissertationen, jedoch nur eine bedeutende wissenschaftliche Studie aus der Feder von Helmut Papajewski an der Berliner Universität, von der bereits in der Kriegszeit ein Kapitel in einer deutschen Zeitschrift veröffentlicht wurde. Als diese Monographie über „die Welt-, Lebens- und Kunstanschauung William Somerset Maughams" 1952 im Kölner Universitätsverlag erschien, war Maugham anfangs so überzeugt von dem Wert dieser Studie, dass er sich um eine Übersetzung ins Englische bemühte. Allerdings wurde der Gedanke bald verworfen, da Maugham bei zunehmender Beschäftigung mit Papajewskis Arbeit seine Enttäuschung nicht verhehlen konnte.

Im Gegensatz zu den bisher genannten Publikationen wurden unsere eigenen Beiträge sowohl in deutscher als auch in englischer Sprache, mehrmals sogar in Tokio veröffentlicht. Maugham hat sich eingehend mit diesen Publikationen befasst und einmal ein Vorwort zu einer biographischen Skizze, *The Gentleman from Cap Ferrat*, beigesteuert. Da sie ausnahmslos seit langem vergriffen sind, haben wir uns entschlossen, zwei an entlegener Stelle veröffentlichte Vorträge einem größeren Leserkreis zugänglich zu machen. Den an der University of Pittsburgh gehaltenen Vortrag „The Maugham Enigma" hat die Japanese Maugham Society 1966 in einer dem Andenken an Maugham gewidmeten Sondernummer der Zeitschrift *The Study of English Literature* im englischen Original mit japanischen Anmerkungen veröffentlicht. Den im Sommer 1972 in deutscher Sprache in Biberach an der Riß gehaltenen Vortrag hat Heinz Sauereßig, der Begründer und langjährige Leiter der Vortragsreihe „Wege und Gestalten" des Pharmakonzerns Dr. Karl Thomae, in dem Band *Universitätstage in Biberach* (1973) herausgegeben.

Eigens für den vorliegenden Band geschrieben wurde das Kapitel „Aus dem Briefwechsel mit Somerset Maugham" mit persönlichen Reminiszenzen des Verfassers dieses Bandes an Maugham und Alan Searle.

Thomas Breitenauer (Technische Universität München) gilt mein aufrichtiger Dank für die Erstellung der Druckvorlage und die harmonische Zusammenarbeit während des vergangenen Jahres. Für ihren Rat, ihre Ermutigung und ihre hilfreichen Vorschläge sage ich Julia Guthmüller vom Lektorat des Harrassowitz Verlags meinen herzlichen Dank.

Sehr zu danken habe ich ebenfalls dem stets hilfsbereiten einstigen Kollegen an der University of Pittsburgh, Thomas F. Staley, dem langjährigen Direktor des Humanities Research Center der University of Texas in Austin, für seine freundliche Unterstützung beim Zustandekommen des vorliegenden Bandes.

Klaus W. Jonas, München, Sommer 2009

Chronicle of Maugham's Life

1874

Birth in the British Embassy in Paris, the sixth and youngest son of Robert Ormond Maugham (1823–1884) and his wife Edith, née Snell. Maugham's father ran the Paris office of his own law firm Maugham et Dixon, additionally serving as advisor and solicitor to the Embassy. A happy, carefree childhood spent in the family home near Rond Point des Champs-Élysées, 25 Ave d'Antin (now Ave. Franklin D. Roosevelt). Summers spent in a rented Villa in Deauville on the Normandy coast. Due to his mother's health problems winters in the mild climate of Pau, a health resort near the Pyrenees.

1882

Maugham never managed to overcome the death of his mother at the age of 41, it remained the greatest loss of his life.

1884

Death of his father from stomach cancer. The ten-year-old orphan sent to Whitstable, Kent, England to his uncle and aunt, an elderly childless couple, the Reverend Henry MacDonald Maugham (1828–1897), an Anglican clergyman, and his German-born wife, Barbara Sophie von Scheidlin. For the next few years the sensitive boy suffered from life with his strict uncle.

1885–89

King's School, Canterbury, Kent.

1888–89

The winters spent recuperating from a lung infection in the mild climate of Huyère in the south of France.

1890–91

Finally young Maugham allowed a year's study abroad attending lectures at Heidelberg University and most impressed by the philosopher Kuno Fischer, lecturing on Schopenhauer. For the first time able to enjoy freedom after the difficult years at King's School in Canterbury where he was teased about his stammer. His attachment to Heidelberg grew with age.

1892

Autumn: Maugham began to study medicine at St. Thomas's Hospital in London.

1894

Spring. First trip to Italy, staying mostly in Florence, also visiting Capri where he would spend many summer months in the following years.

1897

Graduation from St. Thomas's as a Licentiate of the Royal College of Physicians and a member of the Royal College of Surgeons. He later regretted not having served as a doctor for any length of time. Most of his time spent reading and writing.

First modest success as a writer came with the publication of a naturalistic novel *Liza of Lambeth*, the result of his experiences as a doctor in the London slums.

1888–89

December to April: First of many sojourns in Spain, one of his favorite countries, about which he wrote repeatedly. For almost three decades, until settling in France in 1928, he resided in London, working freelance.

1904–05

A year in the Latin Quarter of Paris where he first met his future friend, the painter Gerald Kelly. Each year one unsuccessful novel published. Income from his writings sufficient for his modest life-style.

1906

January to March: Greece and Egypt. Start of a passionate love affair with Ethelwyn (Sue) Jones, the daughter of the author Henry Arthur Jones. The inspiration for his novel *Cakes and Ale*.

1907

First real success as a playwright for the London stage and also for New York with his comedy *Lady Frederick*.

1910

Autumn: First of numerous trips to the United States to visit relatives in Tenafly, New Jersey.

1914–15

Outbreak of First World War: Maugham volunteered to France with the Red Cross as a medic from October 1914 to February 1915. Friendship with Desmond MacCarthy and Gerald Haxton (1892–1944), an American who became his companion and secretary until the end of his life.

February: Return to England.

July to September in Rome with his future wife, Maud Gwendolen Syrie Barnardo, divorced from Henry Wellcome.

September 1 (1915): Birth of daughter Elizabeth (1915–1998) in Rome.

From September through July 1916: As an agent of the British Secret Service, based in Geneva, Switzerland, collecting material for his volume *Ashenden, or the Secret Agent.*

1916

November: With Gerald Haxon, the first long trip to the Far East, visiting San Fransisco, Hawaii, Samoa and Tahiti where he acquired a Gauguin painting. First encounter with Bertram Alanson, later his closest friend and manager of his American portfolio.

1917

Second trip to the United States: May 28, Jersey City, New Jersey. Marriage to Syrie, later a successful interior decorator. In spite of a shared residence in London in the next decade, the couple mostly lived apart until their final separation and divorce.

July 28 to November: Again as British Secret Service agent, this time assigned to Petrograd. Close collaboration with Alexander Kerensky's provisional government. His mission to help prevent the Bolsheviks from taking over, ended in complete failure.

October 22: Shortly before the outbreak of the Russian Revolution, a hasty return to London via Stockholm.

1917–18

The winter months recuperating from tuberculosis in a sanatorium in Nordach-on-Dee near Aberdeen, Scotland.

1918

Summer: Maugham and Syrie in Charles Hill near Farnham (Surrey).

1919–20

September to March: First extended trip to China.

October: New York, Los Angeles and San Francisco.

1921

February to July: Hawaii, Australia, Malaya and Northern Borneo.

1922–23

October to July: Colombo (Ceylon), Burma, Siam and Indochina.

1924–25

September to January: New York, Mexico City, Cuernavaca, Yucatan, Belize, Havana (Cuba), British Honduras, Guatemala.

1926

Summer: Sanitorium in Brides-les-Bains.

1928

Divorce from Syrie – Acquisition of the Villa Mauresque in St. Jean, Cap Ferrat on the French Riviera.

Beginning of life-long friendship with Alan Searle.

1929

Autumn: Greece (Crete, Rhodos) and Egypt.

1930

Elected as Member of the British PEN-Club.

1932

Berlin, Munich, Innsbruck, Würzburg, Vichy, Spain, Portugal.

1934

Spain (Gibraltar, Granada, Sevilla, Tarragona, Valencia), Bad Gastein, Salzburg, Lake Como, Siena.

1935–36

Salzburg, Bad Gastein, Munich, Pressburg (Bratislava), Vienna.

December to January: Haiti, French Guiana including the penal colony of St. Laurent-du-Maroni.

Visits to various Caribbean islands.

July 24: Daughter Elizabeth's (Liza's) marriage to Vincent Paravicini, son of the Swiss ambassador to London.

1937

Copenhagen, Stockholm, Bad Gastein, Salzburg, Vienna.

1938

First of several stays in Paul Niehans' clinic near Vevey on Lake Geneva.

1937–38

May to July: India (Agra, Benares, Bombay, Hyderabad, Calcutta and Madras, New Delhi), Germany, Scandinavia and Switzerland (Vevey).

Maugham's older brother Frederick Herbert became Lord Chancellor acquiring the title „Viscount Maugham of Hartfield".

1939

February to March: United States: New York, Chicago, San Francisco to see Bertram Alanson.

Paris for award of „Commander of the Legion of Honor".

Florence, Lucca, Montecatini.

June 16: Honarary degree awarded by the University of Toulouse under its president, Paul Dottin.

September: Service in the British Ministry of Information.

1940

June 22: Evacuation of all British citizens from the French Riviera. Escape to England via Lisbon.

October 11: Arrival in New York.

October 13: Speeches by both Maugham and Thomas Mann at dinner in Hotel Commodore to welcome newly arrived European refugees, among them Golo Mann, Heinrich Mann, Conrad Heiden and Franz Werfel. The following years to May, 1946, in the United States under an agreement with the British Government.

1941

Life in the United States: Spring and autumn in the Ritz-Carlton Hotel in New York, summer months at the Old Colonial Inn, Edgartown, Martha's Vineyard, Massachusetts.

Summer of 1942 in a rented villa on 732 South Beverly Glen Boulevard, West Los Angeles.

March: Visit with his friend Richard A. Cordell in Lafayette, Indiana, for seminars and discussions with students of Purdue University.

December to 1946: Move into a cottage built for him by his friend and publisher, Nelson Doubleday, on his plantation at Parker's Ferry, Yemassee, South Carolina. The lonely winter months interrupted only by visitors such as his nephew Robin Maugham, his bridge partner Karl G. Pfeiffer, his friend Glenway Wescott and Gerald Haxton who had accepted a clerical position in the U.S. Government in Washington, D.C.

1944

November 7: Death of Gerald Haxton at the age of 52.

A Writer's Notebook dedicated „to his memory".

1945

December: Arrival of Alan Searle (1905–1985) a London social worker in charge of released convicts. Since 1928 regular guest of Maugham's in the Dorchester Hotel on each visit to the British capital. From now on to the end of Maugham's life, he faithfully served as lover-companion, secretary and finally nurse.

1946

April 20: Ceremony in the Library of Congress for the donation of the original manuscript of his novel *Of Human Bondage* as a token of gratitude for the hospitality America had granted him during the war years. During that time Maugham had served the Library as a "Consultant in English Literature".

June: Maugham and Alan Searle returned to the extensively war-damaged Villa Mauresque.

1947

Establishment of the „Somerset Maugham Award" to be administered by the Royal Literary Fund and awarded annually to an English author under 35 who had published at least one literary work.

1948

April: Spain.

June: After divorcing Paravicini, Liza married Lord John Hope, the future Lord Glendevon, son of the Marquis of Linlithgo, a former Viceroy of India.

Together with Thomas Mann's novel *Doctor Faustus*, Maugham's historical novel *Catalina*, his last work of fiction, was part of a dual selection of the Book-of-the-Month Club in New York. 50 000 copies were printed for the Club.

1949

Last reunion with his publisher Nelson Doubleday in New York, followed by a visit to Bertram Alanson in San Francisco.

1950

April: Morocco.

October 17: Appointed „Honorary Associate" by the American Academy of Arts and Letters in New York. Irwin Edman, a professor of philosophy at Columbia University, introduced Maugham and invited him to lecture to his students.

November: Presentation of the original manuscript of "The Artistic Temperament of Stephen Carey" to the Library of Congress. This is the first version of the novel *Of Human Bondage* and was donated to the Library with the stipulation that no part of it will ever be published.

1951

Spain and Portugal.

1952

Awarded an honorary doctorate by Oxford University.

September: Hernia operation in Switzerland.

1953

Farewell trips to Greece and Turkey.

1954

June 9: Private audience with Queen Elizabeth II in Buckingham Palace for his inclusion in the "Queen's Birthday Honours List".

Spain as guest of the Spanish State Tourist Department.

1955

July 28: Death of Syrie Maugham. Unsuccessful attempt to adopt Alan Searle. The district court in Nice turned down his application.

1956

January: Guest of his friend, the Aga Khan, in his villa in Egypt, as a token of appreciation of the preface Maugham had contributed to his memoirs.

Visit with art historian Bernard Berenson in his Villa „I Tatti" near Florence.

1957

May: Visit to his alma mater, the University of Heidelberg, where he signs the "Golden Book" before going to Munich and Bad Gastein.

1958

Death of brother Frederick Herbert Viscount Maugham of Hartfield at the age of 91.

1959–60

April: Munich, Bad Gastein, Vienna and Venice.

Last visit to the Far East: Aden, Bombay, Colombo, Hong Kong, Kobe, Manila, Singapore, Tokyo. Exhibition of Maugham's writings. Establishment of the Japanese Maugham Society, initiated by Mutsuo Tanaka of Tokyo University.

1961

May 31: Awarded an honorary degree as senator of Heidelberg University. Enthusiastic reception by the students.

Honored by the Royal Society of Literature as „Companion of Literature", together with Winston Churchill, Edward M. Forster, John Masefield and George M. Trevelyan.

Donation of his personal library to King's School Canterbury, plus a generous sum for the erection of a special building to house the Maugham Library.

1962

April 10: Maugham's impressive collection of modern paintings was auctioned off by Sotheby's. Proceeds to go to the Royal Literary Fund to augment the annual „Maugham Award".

1964

In his Last Will and Testament of July 9, 1964, Maugham requested that his friends destroy his letters and other personal documents and never assist any future biographer. He also stipulated that his estate be divided between his daughter Lady John Hope and Alan Searle.

1965

September: Last visitor, his old friend Noël Coward. Health deterioration.

December 10: Taken by ambulance to the Anglo-American Hospital in Nice for treatment by his long-time personal physician, Dr. Georges Rosanoff.

Death on December 15. Burial on the grounds of King's School next to Canterbury Cathedral and his library.

1966

After the sale of the Villa Mauresque, Alan Searle with Maugham's last footman moved to an apartment in Monte Carlo for the last twenty years of his life. Constant quarrels with Maugham's daughter over their inheritance.

April: Memorial symposium at the University of California Library in Los Angeles. The speakers included not only members of the English Department but also admirers such as George Cukor, Ruth Gordon and Claire Booth Luce.

1967

The remaining contents of the Villa Mauresque auctioned off by Sotheby & Co. in London.

Leben Somerset Maughams

1874

25. Januar Geburt in der Britischen Botschaft in Paris als sechster und jüngster Sohn des Rechtsanwalts Robert Ormond Maugham (1823 – 1884) und seiner Ehefrau Edith, geborene Snell. Neben seiner Tätigkeit in der eigenen Kanzlei Maugham et Dixon arbeitet sein Vater als Berater der Britischen Botschaft. In der Nähe des Rond Point des Champs-Élysées, 25 ave. d'Antin (heute 25 ave. Franklin D. Roosevelt), verbringt Maugham eine glückliche, sorglose Kindheit. Besuch einer französischen Privatschule.

1882

31. Januar Tod der an Tuberkulose leidenden Mutter im Alter von 41 Jahren. Größter Schmerz in seinem Leben.

1884

Juni Tod des Vaters. Zum ersten Mal im Leben kommt der zehnjährige Junge nach England ins Haus eines kinderlosen Onkels, Reverend Henry Macdonald Maugham, eines anglikanischen Geistlichen, und dessen aus Deutschland stammender Ehefrau Barbara Sophie, einer geborenen von Scheidlin. Im Pfarrhaus in Whitstable in Kent leidet der sensible Junge unter dem von Anfang an gespannten Verhältnis zu seinen Pflegeeltern, vor allem dem ungeliebten Onkel.

1885

Nach dem ersten Jahr in einer öffentlichen Schule kommt Maugham auf die berühmte King's School in Canterbury, wo er, behindert anfangs durch mangelnde Kenntnis in der englischen Sprache und durch einen Sprachfehler, die nächsten fünf Jahre verbringt.

1888–89

Zweimal darf Maugham wegen eines Lungenleidens die Wintermonate im milden Klima von Hyères in Südfrankreich verbringen; seitdem seine lebenslange Liebe zur Französischen Riviera.

1890–91

Immatrikuliert an der Universität Heidelberg, wo er besonders von den Vorlesungen des Philosophen Kuno Fischer beeindruckt ist. Bis zu seinem Lebensende bleibt die glückliche Zeit in Deutschland unvergessen in seiner Erinnerung.

1892

Im Herbst beginnt Maugham das Studium der Medizin am St. Thomas's Hospital in London und genießt die damit verbundene Freiheit nach den schwierigen Jahren als Schüler im Internat in Canterbury.

1894

Im Frühjahr erste Italienreise, längerer Aufenthalt in Florenz und Capri.

1897

Abschluss des Medizinstudiums als Licentiate of the Royal College of Physicians und Member of the Royal College of Surgeons. Den Arztberuf übt er nur wenige Monate aus, verbringt die meiste Zeit mit Lesen und Schreiben.

Erster schriftstellerischer Erfolg mit dem im Armenviertel Londons spielenden naturalistischen Roman *Liza of Lambeth*.

1898

Erster von zahlreichen Aufenthalten in Spanien. Von nun an nur noch als freier Schriftsteller tätig mit Wohnsitz in London bis zu seiner Übersiedlung 1928 nach Südfrankreich.

1904

Bis 1905 verbringt er ein Jahr im Quartier Latin in Paris, Beginn der lebenslangen Freundschaft mit dem Maler Gerald Kelly. Jedes Jahr publiziert Maugham einen wenig erfolgreichen Roman, kann jedoch von seiner schriftstellerischen Tätigkeit einen bescheidenen Lebensstandard aufrecht erhalten. Zum dritten Mal verbringt er die Sommermonate auf Capri.

1906

Im Frühjahr besucht er zum ersten Mal Griechenland und Ägypten.

Beginn des Liebesverhältnisses zu Ethelwyn (Sue) Jones, Tochter des Dramatikers Henry Arthur Jones.

1907

Erster großer Erfolg auf der Londoner Bühne und bald auch in New York mit der Komödie *Lady Frederick*.

1908

Großer Erfolg mit vier seiner Dramen, die gleichzeitig am Londoner West End gespielt werden.

1910

Im Herbst erste von zahlreichen Amerikareisen zum Besuch von Verwandten in Tenafly New Jersey.

1914

Bei Kriegsausbruch geht Maugham freiwillig als Ambulanzfahrer an die französische Front – Beginn der Freundschaft mit Desmond MacCarthy. Begegnung mit dem Amerikaner Gerald Haxton (1892–1944) – Lebenspartner bis zu dessen Tod.

1915

Im Februar Rückkehr nach England, verbringt die Sommermonate zusammen mit seiner späteren Ehefrau Maud Gwendolen Syrie Barnardo, der geschiedenen Frau von Henry Wellcome, in Rom.

1. September: Geburt der Tochter Elizabeth (1915–1998) in Rom.

1915

Bis 1916 Geheimagent des British Secret Service in der Schweiz mit Wohnsitz in Genf (September 1915 bis Juli 1916). Sammelt Material für den Band *Ashenden, or the Secret Agent*.

1916

November: zusammen mit Gerald Haxton erste Ostasienreise. Von nun an sein ständiger Begleiter und Sekretär. Zum ersten Mal besucht Maugham Hawaii, Samoa und Tahiti, wo er ein Gemälde von Gauguin erwirbt. Begegnung mit Bertram Alanson, lebenslange enge Freundschaft mit dem späteren Präsidenten der San Francisco Stock Exchange.

1917

Zweite USA-Reise. Am 26. Mai Eheschließung mit der später als Innenarchitektin bekannten Syrie Barnardo in Jersey City, New Jersey. Im folgenden Jahrzehnt lebt das Ehepaar trotz des gemeinsamen Wohnsitzes in London meist getrennt bis zur endgültigen Trennung.

28. Juli: Beginn der Tätigkeit als Agent im Britischen Geheimdienst in St. Petersburg. Enge Zusammenarbeit mit Alexander Kerensky's provisorischer Regierung.

22. Oktober: Kurz vor Ausbruch der Russischen Revolution überstürzte Rückkehr über Stockholm nach London.

1917

Beide Winter, 1917 und 1918, verbringt Maugham wegen seines Lungenleidens in der Nähe von Aberdeen in einem Sanatorium in Nordach-on-Dee in Schottland.

1918

Sommer: Maugham und Syrie in Charles Hill in der Nähe von Farnham (Surrey).

1919

Verkauf des Hauses 6 Chesterfield Street in London.

August: Einzug in 2 Wyndham Place.

1919–20

Erster längerer Aufenthalt in China.

1920

April: Rückkehr nach England.

Im Herbst Reise nach New York, Los Angeles und San Francisco.

1921

Februar bis Juli: Hawaii, Australien, Malaya und Nord-Borneo.

1922–23

Colombo (Ceylon), Rangun, Mandalay, Siam, Burma, Saigon, Hanoi, Angkor Wat, Indochina.

1924–25

September bis Januar: Mexico City, Cuernavaca, Yucatan, Havana/Cuba, Belize, Britisch-Honduras, Guatemala, New York.

1925

Syrie Maugham tritt hervor als Innenarchitektin. Trotz zunehmender Eheprobleme letzter Besuch als ihr Gast in der Villa Eliza in Le Tourquet.

Sommer: Capri – zur Kur in Brides-les-Bains.

1926

Frühjahr: Hotel Réserve in Beaulieu-sur-mer nach Verkauf seines Londoner Hauses 43 Bryanston Square.

Juni: zur Kur in Brides-les-Bains.

August: Zusammen mit Syrie in Salzburg.

September bis November: New York, Cleveland.

1928

Beginn der Beziehung zum 23-jährigen Alan Searle (1905–1985), der bis 1945 von London aus als Sekretär für Maugham arbeitet.

Scheidung von Syrie, die ihren Mann trotz aller Differenzen bis zum Tod liebt.

August: Einzug in die Villa Mauresque in St. Jean, Cap Ferrat, seinem Domizil bis an sein Lebensende.

Villa Mauresque. In den folgenden Jahren bis zu seinem Ende zahlreiche Gäste aus aller Welt, z.B. Maughams Tochter Liza mit Familie, Gerald Kelly, Bertram Alanson, Charlie Chaplin, Kenneth Clark, Karl G. Pfeiffer, Monroe Wheeler, Garson Kanin, Ruth Gordon, Glenway Wescott, Noël Coward, Godfrey Winn, Beverley Nichols, Cecil Beaton, Winston Churchill, Robin Maugham und Lord Beaverbrook.

Sommer: Zur Kur in Brides-les-Bains.

Herbst: New York.

1929

Kur in Brides-les-Bains.

Herbstreise nach Griechenland, Kreta, Rhodos und Ägypten.

1930

Wahl zum Mitglied des Pen-Club in England auf Vorschlag von H.G. Wells.

1932

Februar: Deutschland (Berlin, Innsbruck, München, Würzburg).

Juli: Kur in Vichy.

September/Oktober: Spanien und Portugal.

1934

März/April: Spanien (Gibralta, Granada, Sevilla, Tarragona, Valencia).

Juli/August: Kur in Bad Gastein, Salzburg, Comer See, Siena.

1935

Juni/Juli: Venedig, Bad Gastein, München, Pressburg (Bratislava), Salzburg, Wien.

Oktober/November: New York – Freundschaft mit Carl Van Vechten – Sea Island (Georgia) – Besuch beim Verleger Nelson Doubleday in Yemassee (South Carolina).

1936

Januar bis April: Französisch Guyana, Besuch der Strafkolonie St.-Laurent-du-Maroni, Curaçao, Cartagena (Columbien), Panama City, Besuch bei Bertram Alanson in San Francisco.

24. Juli: Eheschließung seiner Tochter Elizabeth (Liza) mit Vincent Paravicini, dem Sohn des Schweizer Gesandten in London. Besucht mehrere karibische Inseln.

August/September: Bad Gastein, Budapest, Wien.

1937

August/September: Deutschland und Skandinavien (Kopenhagen, Stockholm, Bad Gastein, Salzburg, Wien).

1937–38

Vom 10. Dezember bis Ende März: Indien (Agra, Benares, Bombay, Calcutta, Hyderabad, Madras, Madura)

1938

Erster Klinikaufenthalt im schweizerischen Vevey am Genfer See zur Behandlung bei Professor Paul Niehans.

Ernennung seines Bruders Frederick zum Lord Chancellor mit dem Titel: „Viscount Maugham of Hartfield."

1939

Februar und März: USA-Reise nach New York, Chicago und San Francisco zum Besuch bei Bertram Alanson.

April: Florenz .

16. Juni: Verleihung der Ehrendoktorwürde der Universität Toulouse durch den Rektor Paul Dottin.

2. August: Ebenfalls in Frankreich wird Maugham ausgezeichnet durch die Verleihung des Titels „Commander of the Legion of Honor".

Kur in Montecatini, Besuch von Florenz und Lucca.

Herbst: Beginn der Tätigkeit für das Britische Informationsministerium. In Straßburg erlebt er zum ersten Mal einen Fliegeralarm.

1940

Frühjahr: Zum ersten Mal im Leben ist Maugham bereit, in London im BBC zu sprechen, was er bisher stets vermieden hatte.

22. Juni: Evakuierung aller britischen Staatsangehörigen von der französischen Riviera – Flucht über Lissabon nach England.

11. Oktober: Ankunft in New York – Im Hotel Commodore hält er am 13. – ebenso wie Thomas Mann – eine Begrüßungsansprache beim Festessen zur Ehrung deutscher Schriftstellerkollegen wie Heinrich und Golo Mann, Konrad Heiden und Franz Werfel. Während der nächsten Jahre hält sich Maugham im Auftrag des britischen Informationsministeriums bis Mai 1946 in den USA auf.

1941

Im Frühjahr und Herbst regelmäßiger Aufenthalt im Ritz-Carlton Hotel in New York, während der Sommermonate alljährlich im Old Colonial Inn, Edgartown, Martha's Vineyard, Massachusetts.

März: Besuch bei seinem Freund Richard A. Cordell in Lafayette, Indiana. Begegnungen und Seminare für Studenten der Purdue University.

Dezember: Einzug in ein von seinem Verleger und Freund Nelson Doubleday gebautes Cottage auf dessen Besitz, Parker's Ferry, Yemassee, South Carolina, wo Maugham die Wintermonate verbringt.

Gelegentliche Besuche von seinem Neffen Robin Maugham, Karl G. Pfeiffer, Glenway Wescott und Gerald Haxton aus Washington.

1942

Sommer: einige Monate in einer gemieteten Villa, 732 South Beverly Glen Boulevard, West Los Angeles.

1944

7. November: Tod seines Lebensgefährten Gerald Haxton im Alter von 52 Jahren. Seinem Andenken widmet er den Band *A Writer's Notebook*.

1945

Dezember: Ankunft des seit 1928 eng befreundeten Alan Searle (1905 – 1985) aus England, der bei jedem Besuch Maughams in England zu Gast im Hotel Dorchester in London weilte und von nun an bis zum Lebensende Maughams Liebhaber, Sekretär und Lebensgefährte wird.

1946

20. April: Zeremonie in der Library of Congress in Washington D.C., der Maugham jahrelang als Consultant in English Literature gedient hatte. Übergabe des Manuskripts seines Entwicklungsromans *Of Human Bondage* (1915) als Zeichen seiner Dankbarkeit für die ihm gewährte Gastfreundschaft während der Kriegsjahre.

Juni: Maugham und Alan Searle kehren in die weitgehend zerstörte Villa Mauresque zurück.

1947

Stiftung des vom Royal Literary Fund verwalteten „Somerset Maugham Award", eines Literaturpreises für ein belletristisches Werk eines englischen Autors unter 35. Unter den Trägern sind bekannte Autoren wie Doris Lessing, V.S. Naipaul, Kingsley Amis, Ted Hughes, Ian McEwan und John le Carré.

In der Royal Society of Literature hält Maugham einen Vortrag über Kipling.

1948

Studienreise nach Spanien in Vorbereitung einer Arbeit über den Maler Zurbarán.

Juni: Ein Jahr nach ihrer Scheidung von Paravicini heiratet Maughams Tochter Liza (Elizabeth) Lord John Hope, den späteren Lord Glendevon, Sohn des Marquis von Linlithgow, vormals Vize-König von Indien.

1948/1950

Maugham spricht im Fernsehen Einleitungen zu seinen Filmen *Quartet*, *Trio* und *Encore*.

1949

Januar: Reise nach New York zum letzten Wiedersehen mit seinem amerikanischen Verleger Nelson Doubleday – Weiterreise nach San Francisco zum Besuch bei Bertram Alanson.

Reise nach Portugal.

Maugham-Portrait von Graham Sutherland gelangt in die Londoner Tate Gallery.

1950

Reise nach Marokko.

17. Oktober: Aufnahme in die American Academy of Arts and Letters in New York als „Honorary Associate". Einführung von Philosophieprofessor Irwin Edman von der Columbia University, an der Maugham eine Vorlesung hält.

Diverse weitere Vorträge während seines letzten USA-Aufenthalts im Leben: In der National Society of Arts and Letters in New York als neugewähltes Mitglied, und in der Pierpont Morgan Library bei einem Dinner ihm zu Ehren.

November: Übergabe des Originalmanuskripts von „The Artistic Temperament of Stephen Carey", des Vorläufers zum Roman *Of Human Bondage,* an die Library of Congress, unter der Bedingung, dass kein Tel dieses Textes jemals veröffentlicht werden dürfe.

1951

Reisen nach Spanien und Portugal.

Oktober: „The Writer's Point of View", Ansprache in der National Book League in Londons Kingsway Hall.

1952

Ehrendoktorwürde der Oxford University.

Oktober: Besuch bei Canon Shirley, Headmaster der King's School in Canterbury.

1953

Frühjahr: Reise in die Türkei und nach Griechenland.

Gast des griechischen Königspaars in Athen.

1954

Frühjahr in Italien und Spanien.

9. Juni: Privataudienz bei Queen Elizabeth II im Buckingham Palace zwecks Auszeichnung durch Aufnahme in die „Queen's Birthday Honours List" anlässlich seines 80. Geburtstages.

In Spanien als Gast des Spanish State Tourist Department.

1955

28. Juli: Tod von Syrie Maugham.

Vergebliche Bemühungen, Alan Searle zu adoptieren – das Gericht in Nizza entscheidet dagegen.

1956

Januar bis Februar: Gast des befreundeten Aga Khan in dessen Villa in Ägypten als Dank für Maughams Vorwort zu dessen Lebenserinnerungen.

1957

Mai: Besuch seiner Alma mater, der Universität Heidelberg, wo er sich in das Goldene Buch einträgt. Weiterreise nach München und Bad Gastein.

1958

Tod des Bruders Frederick Viscount Maugham of Hartfield im Alter von 91 Jahren.

Wahl zum Vize-Präsidenten der Royal Society of Literature, zusammen mit Winston Churchill, Edith Sitwell und Cecil Day-Lewis.

Besuch bei Paul Niehans in seiner Villa in Burier La Tour de Peilz am Genfer See. Auch Konrad Adenauer, Bernard Baruch, Charles de Gaulle, Charlie Chaplin, Marlene Dietrich, Papst Pius XII. sowie Gloria Swanson gehörten zu dessen Patientenkreis.

1959

April: München, Bad Gastein, Wien und Venedig.

1959–60

Ostasienreise – Eröffnung einer Maugham-Ausstellung in Tokio und Gründung einer Japanese Maugham Society.

1961

31. Mai: Ehrensenator der Universität Heidelberg – als einziger Engländer in der Geschichte der Universität.

Höchste Auszeichnung durch die Royal Society of Literature, zusammen mit Winston Churchill, E.M. Forster, John Masefield und George M. Trevelyan als „Companion of Literature".

1962

10. April: Versteigerung von Maughams Impressionistensammlung bei Sotheby in London. Wiederum geht der Erlös an den Royal Literary Fund zwecks Aufstockung des „Somerset Maugham Award".

Herbst: Letzter Aufenthalt in England. Besuch seiner Schule, der Maugham einen Teil seiner privaten Bibliothek vermacht.

1964

In seinem Testament vom 9. Juli 1964 bittet Maugham seine Bekannten und Freunde, Briefe und andere persönliche Dokumente zu vernichten und etwaigen Biographen keinerlei Unterstützung bei ihren Projekten zukommen zu lassen.

Der King's School vermacht er außer seiner umfangreichen Bibliothek ein eigens dafür errichtetes Gebäude, zusammen mit einer großzügigen finanziellen Stiftung. Den Rest seines Vermögens sollen zu gleichen Teilen seine Tochter Lady John Hope sowie Alan Searle erhalten.

1965

September: Als letzten Besucher in der Villa Mauresque empfängt Maugham seinen alten Freund Noël Coward. Zunehmende Verschlechterung seines Gesundheitszustandes.

Am 10. Dezember Überführung ins Anglo-American Hospital in Nizza und Behandlung durch seinen Hausarzt Dr. Georges Rosanoff bis zu seinem Tod am 15. Dezember. Beisetzung im kleinsten Kreise unmittelbar an der Canterbury Cathedral.

1966

April: Gedenkveranstaltung an der Bibliothek der University of California in Los Angeles zu Ehren des verstorbenen Schriftstellers. Unter den Sprechern befanden sich außer denVertretern des Department of English Bekannte aus Film- und Theaterkreisen wie George Cukor, Ruth Gordon und Claire Booth Luce.

Nach seinem Tode übersiedelt Alan Searle, zusammen mit Maughams letztem Butler, in seine Wohnung in Monte Carlo, wo er die folgenden zwanzig Lebensjahre verbringt. Während dieser Zeit Erbstreitigkeiten zwischen Alan Searle und Maughams Tochter.

1967

20. November: Versteigerung des gesamten Inhalts der Villa Mauresque bei Sotheby in London.

The Maugham Enigma

The name of William Somerset Maugham (1874–1965) is known today to every connoisseur of letters all over the world. Most readers, however, are not familiar with his less readily comprehensible personality – the so-called „Maugham enigma" – and with the work, surveyable only with difficulty on account of its variety and range, of this man whose reputation, in the last decades of his long life, as „Dean of English Letters", is scarcely impugned.

Somerset Maugham was the last great professional writer of England. For close to seventy years, from 1897 until his death, he earned his living – in the beginning a very modest one – exclusively by his books. He was not, like so many other authors, simultaneously a publisher, book reviewer, radio lecturer, university professor, or civil servant. During his entire writing career he had been expressing his opinions heedless of whether his fellow men agreed with him or not: „I have gone my own way, with a shrug of my shoulder, following the path I have traced, trying with my work to fill out the pattern of life that I have made for myself." There are not many works in the English language which make fewer concessions to their readers than *The Moon and Sixpence, Cakes and Ale,* and *For Services Rendered.*

Maugham had been one of the most versatile writers of his generation who has produced work of a high quality in almost every genre except for lyrical poetry for which, however, he has expressed the highest regard: „I have no doubt that poetry is the highest achievement of the human mind and the writer of prose is not to be considered in the same breath as the poet. It is the poet alone who can achieve beauty." – Maugham has written a total of twenty-three plays, all produced and published, apart from six more which have not been printed, but have been performed repeatedly. He is the author of twenty-four novels, twelve volumes of short stories, a number of travel books (*The Land of the Blessed Virgin* (1905), *On a Chinese Screen* (1922), *The Gentleman in the Parlour* (1930), *Don Fernando* (1935)), autobiographical writings (*The Summing Up* (1938), *A Writer's Notebook* (1949), *Looking Back* (1962)), and several volumes of essays on art, literature, and philosophy, not to mention the wealth of tales and articles which appeared only in journals; and he is the English translator of a few works in French and Italian. Maugham is also one of the outstanding mediators between individual literatures and, as a talented critic and anthologist, has acquainted countless readers with what he considered the best of modern literature, European as well as American. Suffice it to mention here: his collection of essays, *Great Novelists and Their Novels* (1948), and his anthology, *Tellers of Tales* (1939), with its sub-title: '100 Short Stories from the United States, England, France, Russia, and Germany'.

It is well known that Oscar Wilde published his *Salomé* in French and that Joseph Conrad, the Polish exile from the Ukraine, learned his English only as an adult but then attained an uncommen mastery of it. But what fantasy can imagine an Englishman who spoke French as his mother tongue before he even learned English, and then wrote his first dramatic work in German! Yet Somerset Maugham had this oddity on his conscience, and his one-act play *Schiffbrüchig* (Shipwrecked), produced in Berlin in 1902 and later published in English as *Marriages are made in Heaven* in the London yearbook *The Venture,* has deservedly become a literary rarity.

One who, like Somerset Maugham, could look back upon a long, lively, and sometimes adventurous life, will – to put it crudely – have a few stories to tell. The youth, who was born the son of a solicitor assigned to the British Embassy in Paris, spent the first ten years of his life in the cosmopolitan atmosphere of the French capital. After the loss of his parents, his uncle, the Reverend Henry MacDonald Maugham, and his aristocratic German-born wife, took the orphan, who suffered throughout his life from a bad stammer, into their parsonage in Kent and later sent him to the famous King's School in Canterbury, among whose alumni Christopher Marlowe and Sir Hugh Walpole are also numbered. At seventeen Maugham went to Heidelberg University for a year, where he heard lectures by the philosopher Kuno Fischer. After his return to England he studied medicine at St. Thomas's Hospital in London where he passed his medical examination five years later. Of his years as a medical student Maugham writes in *The Summing Up:* „In those years I must have witnessed pretty well every emotion of which man is capable ... I saw how men died. I saw how they bore pain. I saw what hope looked like, fear and relief; I saw the dark lines that despair drew on the face; I saw courage and steadfastness. I saw faith shine in the eyes of those who trusted in what I could only think was an illusion and I saw the gallantry that made a man greet the prognosis of death with an ironic joke because he was too proud to let those about him see the terror of his soul ... The experience of all the years that have followed has only confirmed the observations on human nature that I made, not deliberately, for I was too young, but unconsciously, in the outpatient's department and in the wards of

St. Thomas's Hospital. I have seen men since as I saw them then, and thus have I drawn them." Maugham regretted that he did not practice medicine for any length of time. He believed that his failure to do so had deprived him of many significant experiences which would later have been valuable for his work. „So far as I personally am concerned," he later remarked, „I can only wish that I had remained a doctor for three or four years instead of writing books which have long been as dead as mutton."

Maugham began his literary career not as a dramatist, but as a novelist, and his novels, undoubtedly, are better than his plays because he always took them more seriously. Even his first published work, the naturalistic novel *Liza of Lambeth* (1897), established him as a man of letters with some authority. He knew the life of the London slums well enough to be able to present a deep insight into the abysses and degradations of humanity. At the time of its first publication, it was labelled by some reviewers as „relentlessly realistic, although the squalor of this little book is often positively nauseating." But one of the French critics early detected that it was „a brave novel, written soberly, with direct, simple action."

During the next decade Maugham wrote an average of one novel per year – surely none of them masterpieces – but sustained himself only with difficulty. After a year in Paris he applied himself more energetically to the theater and wrote stage works which soon caught the attention of Max Beerbohm who had succeeded George Bernard Shaw as drama critic of the *Saturday Review*. In 1907, at the age of thirty-three, Maugham experienced for the first time the great material success for which he had been waiting and which subsequently favoured him throughout his entire life. He had always had a healthy respect for money which, he claimed, is „like the sixth sense without which you cannot make use of the other five." And years later, he once wrote into one of his books: „He heard people speak contemptuously of money; he wondered if they had ever tried to do without it." For a while, he had four of his plays – *Lady Frederick, Mrs. Dot, Jack Straw*, and *The Explorer* – running at the same time on London's Strand, and a cartoon in *Punch* pictured Shakespeare looking at the London theater programs envious of Maugham's success. In the years since 1908 he came more and more into contact with the upper middle classes whose life, henceforth, he exposed with great candor in his dramatic works. In many of the plays written between 1903 and 1933, he continued the tradition of the English comedy of manners which had reached its peak in the Restoration period with the works of Congreve, Wycherley and Sheridan. His plays fall into three clearly-marked categories: he started out writing light comedies, achieving his first great success in 1907 with *Lady Frederick.* Later he wrote those comedies in which he revealed the cynicism, particularly in connection with the problem of marriage, that critics have often attributed to him (*Caesar's Wife, The Circle,* and *The Constant Wife*). And finally, until he gave up playwriting altogether in the early thirties, he produced those dramatic works which were marked by their deepening bitterness (*For Services Rendered* and *Sheppey*). In the last-mentioned play, as critic St. John Ervine had pointed out, one discerns the voice of „that generous-minded and socially-indignant doctor" which was to be found in Maugham's first novel, *Liza of Lambeth.*

At the beginning of the First World War, Maugham went to France with the Red Cross and became an ambulance driver with the British Expeditionary Corps, but after only a few months he was assigned as an agent to the Secret Service. For some time he worked in Switzerland for the British Intelligence Office, and after a trip to America and the South Pacific, he was sent in 1917 on a secret mission to Russia to influence the Menshevik Party to continue the war against Germany. He has described his experiences and observations in his popular *Ashenden* stories, which Dr. Goebbels, Minister of Propaganda in Nazi Germany, was to put on his black list some twenty years later.

Before Maugham undertook his great journeys, before he discovered in the problems of race and atmosphere the element which most closely corresponds to his thinking, the shadows of the preternatural wove eerily in his works. There is the early tale *The Magician* (1908), which so intensifies the motif of the incomprehensible union of two lovers who actually hate each other that their relationship becomes an occult phenomenon. In *Of Human Bondage* (1915) Maugham transcends his previous works and succeeds on a grand scale: A hard core of reality underlies this novel of educational development, permeated with autobiographical elements and plotted majestically, which tells the story of the club-footed medical student Philip Carey. „Fact and fiction are inextricably mixed," Maugham would later confess. „The emotions are my own, but not all the incidents related as they happened." Here, in *Of Human Bondage,* too, the concept of reality is dominated by the idea of the predestined relationship of the helpless man to a woman who personifies the irrational beast. And this line of development is continued, for in *The Painted Veil* (1925) Maugham depicts the metamorphosis of this beast into a human being. A cholera epidemic effects this miracle in the adulterous wife of an English bacteriologist living in China. And finally the painter Strickland in *The Moon and Sixpence* (1919) is a beast, albeit a beast possessed by art: In his later years he suddenly turns his back upon his bourgeois profession as a stock broker, leaves his home and family forever, and drags himself with a demonic will through every conceivable morass until, externally, he perishes miserably as a leper on a South Sea island but has imbued his pictures with the true spirit of life: Gauguin's destiny.

Yet these accomplishments, despite their qualitative pre-eminence, seem to be almost nothing more than a prelude in comparison with the artistic form for which Maugham seemed to be pronouncedly destined, although he came to it late: the short story. These stories, almost all of which take place against a background of the Eastern tropics, are frequently transmuted by the capacity of the born dramatist into a form greatly approximating that of the one-act-play. And here, perhaps, is most strongly revealed that effect of French Realism, especially of Guy de Maupassant, which is occasionally ascribed to him. Even the titles of the two collections later reprinted in the volume *East and West*, *The Trembling of a Leaf* (1921) and *The Casuarina Tree* (1926), tell much about concept and motif of the works. In accordance with the famous dictum of Sainte-Beuve, Maugham believes that happiness and grief are so closely related in mankind that even the trembling of a leaf suffices to cause one to reverse into its opposite. But the Casuarina tree, whose growth engenders fertility in the soil of the swamp land and, yet, which is destined to succumb to the powerfully encroaching maze of the jungle, whispers weird things to men at night.

These tales tell of men, races, and social strata in their peculiar, distrustful, tyrannical and fearful relations with one another and with the nervous atmosphere of tropic fate: They tell of the European who takes a native woman into his house and gradually succumbs, in his standards of life, to the dark race; of the upstart who meets the stranded gentleman; of the mongrel who belongs to both races and yet to neither; and of the white woman who breaks down under the certainty that her husband or lover has previously been in erotic intercourse with the other race. A humid, colorful atmosphere, endless steamship journeys, exotic meals in remote bungalows, tedious inspection trips into the unknown interior – all these provide the setting for the passionate actions of the characters. This is also the background of the story *Rain*, which in dramatized form has made its way almost across the entire Continent of Europe, North and South America, and has become perhaps the best known of Maugham's works: the story of that fanatical missionary who, in his attempt to convert a prostitute, is seduced by her and cuts his own throat in despair – „melodramatic", indeed, yet somehow justified in the enervating and rain-surfeited atmosphere of the Pacific Ocean.

Since the Twenties, when Maugham undertook most of his South Sea journeys, and portrayed his experiences from the world *East of Suez* in this and other works – *On a Chinese Screen* (1922), *The Gentlemen in the Parlour* (1930), *The Narrow Corner* (1932), *Ah King* (1933) – since that time his particular interest has been reserved for the Far East. What Maugham thinks of travelling and, above all, what the lands of the Orient have signified for him is reported in his notebooks – he protests against the word „diary" and asserts that he has never kept one – from which he has shown the public but a small selection in *A Writer's Notebook* (1949). The Far East and South America he considered as the lands which he would like to recommend to people with a good gift for observation. But even there, he says, it is no longer easy to find new material since transportation facilities have become so much better in recent years. By the „South Seas" one formerly meant Tahiti and Samoa. But now, Maugham believed, one would have to seek out regions like the islands around Australia and the Malay Peninsula: remote outposts where men are cut off from all civilization for years. But above all it is India which – in his opinion – still conceals untapped wealth. On his journeys Maugham avoided Englishmen whenever possible and sought, by letters of recommendation, to acquire access to the courts of princes and the houses of the wise. There, as soon as the Indians discovered that he did not come to them as a merchant, he encountered more hospitality and ready help than anywhere else.

When Maugham was weary of wandering and made up his mind finally to establish a domicile, he acquired the Villa Mauresque on Cap Ferrat between Nice and Monaco. From 1928 until 1940, and again from 1946 to his death in December, 1965, he lived on his property on the French Riviera, interrupted only by the six years from 1940 to his return after the war, when he was living in the United States in the commission of the British government. In 1944 there appeared one of his most popular novels, *The Razor's Edge*, which has subsequently been filmed in Hollywood; in 1946 the historical novel *Then and Now,* which takes place in the Italy of Machiavelli; in 1947 a collection of short stories, *Creatures of Circumstance*; in 1948 a final novel, *Catalina*, which – together with Thomas Mann's novel, *Doctor Faustus* – became a dual selection of the „Book-of-the-Month Club" in New York.

The last work published during Maugham's lifetime was a *Catalogue of the Collection of Impressionist and Modern Pictures formed by W. Somerset Maugham over the last Fifty Years* (London, 1962), containing illustrations of some thirty-five of his paintings sold at auction at Sotheby's in London on

April 10, 1962. For fear of theft Maugham followed the advice given him by the Mayor of St. Jean to do something about his collection, but instead of building a strong room in his house, he decided to sell them and to turn over the proceeds to the Royal Literary Fund to support needy writers in old age. „Even if I were only going out to dinner I could not be sure," Maugham wrote in his brief preface, announcing the reasons that had prompted his intention, „that a thief would not take the opportunity to steal one or two of my pictures. For many years they had given me great pleasure; now they were an anxiety ... I hope that you will get as much pleasure out of such as you buy tonight as I have got out of them in the past."

The question has often been asked what Maugham's literary rank will be. He himself had no doubt about the place in the history of English letters that posterity may assign to him: he felt that he belonged in the very front row of the second-raters. „I think that one or two of my comedies will be remembered for a time, and a few of my best short stories will find their way into anthologies. This is not much but it is better than nothing."

During most of his life the critics have not been very kind to him: „In my twenties they said I was brutal, in my thirties they said I was flippant, in my forties they said I was cynical, in my fifties they said I was competent, and then, in my sixties, they said I was superficial," Maugham wrote in *The Summing Up*.

„It has happened to me from time to time to run into some person of taste who tells me that I ought to take Somerset Maugham seriously. Yet I have never been able to convince myself that he was anything but second-rate ... My experience with Maugham has always been that he disappoints my literary appetite and so discourages me from going on." Thus wrote the American critic Edmund Wilson who feels that Maugham „is for our day what Bulwer-Lytton was for Dickens': a half-hashy novelist, who writes badly, but is patronized by half-serious readers who do not care much about writing." Gerald Sykes, who admires Maugham's enormous gifts as a craftsman, suggests that sinister influences vitiated his abilities. „What metamorphosis took place? Were his desires worldly from the start, was he fired originally with no artist's longing to see and make, but with an earthling's lust to dine well and glitter? Or was a man of genius, a virgin heart, seduced by the great world of riches and power? Woe to thee, Babylon, that mighty city!" I know of no critic who has less respect for Maugham than Morton Dauwen Zabel who, in reviewing one of his lighter novels, quotes Mr. Clifton Fadiman as saying that „it does not contain a wasted word," only to conclude by adding: „The fact has seldom been more deftly reversed – *all* the words are wasted."

On the other hand there are those serious critics who believe in Maugham's permanent place in literature. Their roster includes such names as W.H. Auden, S.N. Behrman, Cyril Connolly, Richard A. Cordell, Paul Dottin, Theodore Dreiser, St. John Ervine, Ludwig Lewisohn, Harold Nicolson, Helmut Papajewski, V.S. Pritchett, Frank Swinnerton, and Glenway Wescott. Maugham himself was somewhat amused by his growing fame and, in an interview in 1958, stated: „I have found that longevity counts more than talent." Almost quoting from his own favorite among his novels, *Cakes and Ale* (1930), he continued: „You know how funny the English are about old age. Once they take someone to their hearts, they are loyal to the last, whether it's a singer who has lost his voice or an actor who forgets his lines. That seems to have happened to me."

Of all the adjectives used by his critics, none has hurt him more than the charge of cynicism which he considered unjustified. „All I have done was to bring to prominence certain traits that many writers shut their eyes to. It has amused me that the most incongruous traits should exist in the same person – crooks who are capable of self-sacrifice, harlots for whom it was a point of honor to give good value for money. I cannot bring myself to judge my fellows. I am content to observe them."

Another charge made against him by a good many critics who did not take him seriously was their view of him as a „mere story teller." When Maugham was honored by the American Academy of Arts and Letters in New York, he answered those critics by stating his concept of the purpose of the novel: „The novel" he said in his address at the dinner on October 17, 1950, „is a form of art, perhaps not a very exalted one, but a form of art nevertheless. It is not concerned with reform. It offers entertainment and if it is a good novel it offers intelligent entertainment. People who are interested in juvenile delinquency, the prison system and so forth would be better advised to read the books written about them by the experts on these particular subjects. The proper aim of the novelist is to create characters and devise a story which will enable him to display them. If you like to call him a mere story teller of course you are at liberty to do so ... The point I want to make is that the story teller by the nature of his gift, by his peculiar feeling for the circumstances of his time, by his choice of people to write about, by the kind of stories he tells offers a criticism of life. He may not know he is doing this, it may be far from his intention, but he does it willy-nilly. My conclusion is that there is no such thing as a mere story teller."

During all his adult life Maugham has felt the urge to write. „It has been borne in upon me that a good many people are angry with me because my various works have brought me in a great deal of money. That is silly. They ought rather to be angry with the people all over the world who buy my books and pay to go to see my plays. I have written because I had a fertile invention and the ideas for plays and stories that thronged my brain would not let me rest till I had got rid of them by writing them. But that," he wrote to me on May 14, 1956, at the age of eighty-two, „is a thing of the past. With age one's inventiveness leaves one and it is long since I have been troubled with any subject that insisted on being turned into a piece of fiction." And he concluded the letter by adding: „I am well aware that I have lost any talent I may have had. There was only one thing for me to do – to turn critic."

There can be little doubt that it is as a story teller – one of the most productive, most popular and successful ones of this century – that Somerset Maugham has given pleasure to millions of readers all over the world and will continue to do so for many years to come.

Der Gentleman von Cap Ferrat

Mit Somerset Maugham hat es seine eigene Bewandtnis. Sein Name ist zwar jedem Literaturfreund in aller Welt bekannt, weniger vertraut jedoch sind die meisten seiner Leser mit der nicht leicht zu verstehenden Persönlichkeit dieses Schriftstellers und seinem nach Mannigfaltigkeit und Umfang nur noch schwer überschaubaren Werk. Mehr als 60 seiner fast 92 Lebensjahre (25. Januar 1874 – 16. Dezember 1965) hat er aktiv am literarischen Leben seiner Zeit teilgenommen und sich als scharfer, objektiver, geradezu klinischer Beobachter seiner Mitmenschen sowie als glänzender Erzähler weltweiten Ruhm erworben. Skepsis, Ironie, Satire, daneben Toleranz, Humor, und nicht selten auch echtes Mitgefühl, kennzeichnen seine Kunst ebenso, wie die pointierten Betrachtungen der Widersprüchlichkeit und Unberechenbarkeit des menschlichen Handelns. Maugham wollte, wie er selbst einmal bekannte, niemals mehr sein als ein „Geschichtenerzähler", „a story teller", erreichte darin aber eine solche unumstrittene Meisterschaft, dass er es zum vielfachen Millionär brachte.

Somerset Maugham, einer alten berühmten englischen Juristenfamilie entstammend, gilt als einer der letzten großen Berufsschriftsteller seines Landes. Über ein halbes Jahrhundert lang hat er seinen Lebensunterhalt (obwohl, wie seine Kollegen Arthur Conan Doyle, Archibald Joseph Cronin und Arthur Schnitzler von Hause aus Arzt) ausschließlich durch seine Bücher verdient. Er war nicht, wie so viele andere Autoren unter seinen Zeitgenossen, gleichzeitig Verleger, Rezensent, Radiosprecher, Hochschullehrer oder Staatsbeamter. Unbekümmert darum, ob seine Mitmenschen ihm zustimmten oder nicht, hat er durch mehr als sechs Jahrzehnte seine Ansichten freimütig und mit erstaunlicher Offenheit geäußert. In seinen Werken bemerkt der aufmerksame Leser seine unbedingte Aufrichtigkeit bei aller schonungslosen Darstellung menschlicher Schwächen.

In den zwei Jahrzehnten unserer persönlichen Bekanntschaft war es mir vergönnt, Maugham viele Male zu begegnen, des öfteren in New York, am häufigsten in seiner Villa Mauresque am Cap Ferrat oder an anderen Orten der französischen Riviera. Seine Stimme war die eines klugen, gütigen Menschen, sein Blick aber verriet, dass er sich wenig Illusionen über sich und seine Mitmenschen machte. Im Gegensatz zu vielen anderen berühmten Persönlichkeiten sprach er nur selten, und nie unaufgefordert, über sich und sein Werk. In einer größeren Gesellschaft würde man ihn kaum bemerkt haben, hätte aber sicher sein können, von ihm beobachtet zu werden.

Außer 23 veröffentlichten Bühnenstücken hat Maugham sechs weitere geschrieben, die zwar nicht gedruckt, wohl aber wiederholt gespielt wurden. Er ist der Verfasser von 24 Romanen und mehr als 100 Kurzgeschichten, von denen nicht wenige Millionenauflagen erreicht haben; er hat mehrere philosophische Arbeiten, Reiseaufzeichnungen, Vorworte, autobiographische Schriften sowie zahlreiche, großenteils in Buchform gesammelte Essays über Literatur und Kunst geschrieben, abgesehen von einer Fülle nur verstreut in englisch-amerikanischen Zeitschriften erschienene Artikel. Seine letzten, kurz vor seinem Tode geschriebenen, skandalumwitterten Lebenserinnerungen, *Looking Back*, sind zwar niemals als Buch herausgekommen, jedoch in Lord Beaverbrooks Londoner Zeitung *Daily Express* sowie der amerikanischen Zeitschrift *Show* von ungezählten Lesern geradezu verschlungen worden. Maugham hat sich außerdem als Übersetzer aus dem Italienischen und dem Französischen betätigt, und vor allem in Amerika hat er verschiedene angesehene Anthologien herausgebracht. Ich darf hier nur an den über 1500 Seiten starken, in Europa so gut wie unbekannten Band *Tellers of Tales* erinnern, der 1939 kurz vor Kriegsausbruch in New York erschienen war und dessen Untertitel etwas über Maughams Vertrautheit mit der europäischen und amerikanischen Literatur aussagt: „100 Short Stories from the United States, England, France, Russia, and Germany". Was mag er, so wird sich mancher unter Ihnen fragen, damals als das Beste aus der modernen deutschen Prosa ausgewählt haben? Unter den deutschen bzw. österreichischen Autoren, die hier vertreten sind, findet man Arthur Schnitzler und Jakob Wassermann, Hugo von Hofmannsthal und Franz Werfel, Ludwig Thoma, Heinrich Mann und seinen Bruder Thomas Mann, letzteren mit seiner Erzählung aus dem München der Inflationszeit, *Unordnung und frühes Leid*, auf englisch bekannt als *Early Sorrow*.

Die Mehrzahl von Maughams Schriften ist in über 25 Sprachen übersetzt. Man schätzt, dass sich bereits zu seinen Lebzeiten seine Werke einschließlich aller fremdsprachigen Ausgaben in mehr als hundert Millionen Exemplaren verkauft haben.

Doch es hat etwas Merkwürdiges mit diesem kaum zu überbietenden Massenerfolg, der in unserem Jahrhundert bisher – wenigstens auf dem Gebiete der englischen Literatur – nur noch von demjenigen George Bernard Shaws erreicht wurde. Künstlerisches Schaffen und finanzieller Erfolg sollten im Falle Somerset Maughams bis in sein Alter hinein umstritten bleiben, fast als wären sie unvereinbar. Die literarische Kritik seines eigenen Landes hat lange Zeit streng über sein Werk zu Gericht gesessen. Bis in die dreißiger Jahre hat sie sich geweigert, ihn ernst zu nehmen und dem Schriftsteller den ihm gebührenden Rang zu gewähren, obwohl bereits 1908, als vier seiner Theaterstücke gleichzeitig auf den Bühnen der englischen Hauptstadt gespielt wurden, das Witzblatt *Punch* eine Karikatur brachte, auf der Shakespeare voller Neid den Spielplan der Londoner Theater studierte. Der damals einsetzende materielle Erfolg hat ihn bis an sein Lebensende nicht mehr verlassen.

In seiner realistischen Art hat Maugham selbst freimütig zu diesem Phänomen, das heißt der Abneigung der Kritiker ihm gegenüber, Stellung genommen:

„In my twenties the critics said I was brutal; in my thirties they said I was flippant; in my forties they said I was cynical; in my fifties they said I was competent, and then in my sixties they said I was superficial."

„Als ich 20 war, sagten die Kritiker, ich sei brutal; als ich 30 war, hieß es, ich sei vorlaut; als ich 40 war, ich sei zynisch; als ich 50 war, ich sei hinreichend zulänglich, und jetzt, in meinen Sechzigern sagen sie, ich sei oberflächlich."

Obwohl Maughams Stellung im zeitgenössischen Schrifttum längst als gesichert gilt, ist man doch versucht, die anfängliche Ablehnung durch die englische Kritik mit derjenigen anderer literarischer Berühmtheiten zu vergleichen, die ebenfalls im fremden Sprachgebiet lange Zeit höher gewertet wurden als im eigenen. Ich denke z.B. an die Stellung Heinrich Heines in England und USA, an Lord Byrons Beliebtheit in Deutschland, an Charles Morgans Ruhm in Frankreich. Man erinnert sich auch an das merkwürdige Schicksal der Romane Daniel Defoes, die, wie sein *Robinson Crusoe* (1719, zur Zeit ihres Erscheinens überhaupt nicht als Literatur angesehen wurden, oder an einen anderen Engländer, Anthony Trollope, der sich zwar zu Lebzeiten eines bedeutenden Publikumserfolges erfreute, aber erst ein halbes Jahrhundert nach seinem Tode als Gestalter viktorianischen Lebensgefühls voll gewürdigt wurde.

Es ist also keineswegs immer so, dass bei einer ausgesprochenen Diskrepanz zwischen Publikumserfolg und kritischer Zurückhaltung die letztere schließlich recht behalten muß. Ein gewisses Mißtrauen gegenüber der Zuverlässigkeit des Urteils der Kritik – das zeigt sich gerade im Falle Somerset Maughams besonders deutlich – scheint also durchaus gerechtfertigt. Doch es berührte geradezu als peinlich, dass man ihn in England Jahrzehnte lang nur als brillanten, raffinierten Unterhaltungsschriftsteller einschätzte, dem mehr an materiellem Erfolg als an künstlerischem Rang gelegen zu sein schien, als bedeutende Kritiker in anderen Ländern sich bereits ernstlich mit seinen Schriften auseinandersetzten. Erst in späten Jahren also endete die Diskrepanz zwischen Massenerfolg auf der einen und Mißachtung durch die Kritiker auf der anderen Seite, und es konnte nur noch komisch wirken, wie die englische Fachkritik Maughams längst eingetretenen Weltruhm nachträglich gutzuheißen suchte, als bereits hohe und höchste Auszeichnungen ihm zuteil geworden waren. Bis in sein hohes Alter war Maugham zum Beispiel von der Richtigkeit seines vielzitierten Ausspruches überzeugt, den die erbitterte Kritik ihm so oft zum Vorwurf gemacht hatte: „Money is like the sixth sense, without which one cannot make use of the other five." Maugham selbst – das muß zu seiner Verteidigung betont werden – hat den Mut gehabt, sich nie um die Meinungen seiner Kritiker zu kümmern. Allen Anfeindungen und Beschuldigungen zum Trotz, er habe seit dem Erfolg von *Of Human Bondage* (1915 nur noch um des Geldes willen geschrieben, obwohl er seinen Lesern eigentlich gar nichts mehr zu sagen gehabt hätte, ist er seinen eigenen Weg gegangen.

„I have gone my own way" – antwortete er ihnen – „with a shrug of my shoulder, following the path I have traced, trying with my work to fill out the pattern of life that I have made for myself."

Es ist bekannt, dass Oscar Wilde seine *Salomé* zuerst auf Französisch herausbrachte und dass der aus der Ukraine stammende Exilpole Joseph Conrad sein Englisch als Erwachsener neu erlernen mußte, ehe er es dann aber zu einer ungewöhnlichen Meisterschaft brachte. Welche Phantasie aber kann sich einen Engländer vorstellen, der als Muttersprache Französisch spricht, bevor er seine eigene Sprache zu erlernen beginnt, und der dann seinen dramatischen Erstling in deutscher Sprache verfaßt? Diese Absonderlichkeit hat kein anderer als der geheimnisvolle Somerset Maugham auf dem Gewissen. Nicht zu Unrecht ist sein 1902 in Berlin uraufgeführter Einakter *Schiffbrüchig* – später erst unter dem Titel *Marriages are made in Heaven (Ehen werden im Himmel geschlossen)* in der Londoner Zeitschrift *The Venture* erschienen – eine literarische Rarität ersten Ranges geworden.

In Paris als Sohn eines angesehenen englischen Rechtsanwalts geboren, verbringt Maugham in der weltoffenen Atmosphäre der französischen Hauptstadt seine ersten zehn Lebensjahre. Immer wieder hat er später betont, dass Frankreich ihn in vieler Hinsicht, nicht zuletzt als Schriftsteller, beeinflußt, ja geradezu geprägt habe: „Es hat mich gelehrt, Schönheit, Witz, guten Geschmack zu schätzen. Frankreich hat mir die Kunst des Schreibens beigebracht." Durch persönliches Leid früh vereinsamt, geht der zehnjährige

Junge nach dem Tode beider Eltern zu einem mit einer deutschen Aristokratin verheirateten Onkel nach England in ein puritanisches Pfarrhaus in der Grafschaft Kent, später besucht er, durch einen schweren Sprachfehler von seinen Mitschülern isoliert, die berühmte King's School in Canterbury. Bis zu seinem Tode fühlte er sich ihr eng verbunden, und es ist kein Zufall, dass er dieser Schule neben diversen anderen großzügigen Stiftungen seine umfangreiche Bibliothek vermacht hat. Heute befindet sich sein Grab im Park der King's School unweit der Kathedrale von Canterbury.

Mit 17 Jahren geht Maugham als Student nach Heidelberg, um dort Vorlesungen zu hören. Vor allem beeindruckten ihn die Ausführungen des Philosophen Kuno Fischer über Arthur Schopenhauer, der bald zu seinem Lieblingsschriftsteller wird. Dieses Studienjahr in Deutschland (1891–1892) hat Maugham wiederholt als das glücklichste Jahr seines Lebens bezeichnet, und als ich ihm zu seinem 74. Geburtstag 1948 einen Bildband über die Stadt am Neckar schenkte, schrieb er mir in seinem Dankesbrief: „The pictures of Heidelberg made me feel very sentimental".

In seinem Buch *The Summing Up (Rückblick auf mein Leben)* schreibt Maugham ausführlich über seine Berufswahl sowie die Bedeutung des Medizinstudiums für sein Leben und sein Werk als Schriftsteller:

„Als ich mit 18 Jahren aus Deutschland zurückkam, hatte ich meine ganz eigenen und entschlossenen Ansichten über meine Zukunft. Ich war glücklicher gewesen als je zuvor, ich hatte zum ersten Mal den Begriff ‚Freiheit' kennengelernt, und ich konnte den Gedanken, in das Joch von Cambridge zu gehen und die vielen Einschränkungen, die damit verbunden waren, zu erleiden, nicht ertragen. Ich fühlte mich wie ein erwachsener Mann und hatte das eine große Verlangen, sofort in das reale Leben einzutreten. Ich fühlte, ich hätte nicht einen Augenblick zu verlieren.

Der Beruf des Mediziners interessierte mich gar nicht, aber das Studium gab mir die Möglichkeit, in London zu leben und so jene Lebenserfahrung gewinnen zu können, nach der ich so sehr strebte. Im Herbst 1892 trat ich in das St. Thomas's Hospital ein. Die ersten zwei Jahre meines Lebens dort fand ich äußerst langwierig, und ich schenkte meiner Arbeit nicht mehr Aufmerksamkeit, als unbedingt zum Bestehen der Prüfungen nötig war. Ich war ein unbefriedigender Student, aber ich hatte die Freiheit, nach der ich mich sehnte. Ich liebte es, meine eigenen Zimmer zu haben ... Meine gesamte freie Zeit, die ich dem Studium hätte widmen sollen, verbrachte ich mit Lesen und Schreiben. Ich las enorm viel; ich füllte Notizbücher mit Entwürfen zu Geschichten und Theaterstücken, mit Dialogskizzen und Überlegungen ... Am Leben des Spitals nahm ich kaum Anteil und befreundete mich mit wenigen Mitstudenten ... Aber als ich nach zwei Jahren Assistent in der Abteilung für ambulante Patienten wurde, wuchs mein Interesse. Nach einiger Zeit wurde ich diensthabender Arzt und meine Anteilnahme nun so rege, dass ich es einmal nicht erwarten konnte, wieder meine Pflichten zu übernehmen, als ich durch eine Blutvergiftung, die ich mir bei der Sezierung einer stark verwesten Leiche zugezogen hatte, ans Bett gefesselt war. Ich hatte, um ein bestimmtes Zertifikat zu erlangen, dienstlich zahlreichen Niederkünften beizuwohnen, und diese Pflicht führte mich in die Elendsviertel von Lambeth, oft in so schmutzige Höfe und Löcher, dass selbst die Polizei hineinzugehen zögerte; aber meine schwarze Arzttasche schützte mich. Diese Arbeit nahm mich sehr stark in Anspruch, und als ich dann eine Zeitlang auf der Unfallstation, Tag und Nacht, tätig war, um in dringenden Fällen Erste Hilfe zu leisten, war ich zwar körperlich vollkommen übermüdet, aber seelisch wundervoll befriedigt.

Denn hier war ich mit dem unmittelbaren Leben in engstem Kontakt, etwas, was ich immer ersehnt hatte. In diesen drei Jahren muß ich wohl durch alle Gefühlsskalen durchgegangen sein, die ein Mensch passieren kann. Das gefiel meinem dramatischen Instinkt. Das regte den Romanschriftsteller in mir an. Selbst heute, da 40 Jahre vergangen sind, kann ich mich gewisser Menschen so genau erinnern, dass ich sie zeichnen könnte. Sätze, die ich damals hörte, klingen noch immer in meinen Ohren. Ich sah Menschen sterben. Ich sah, wie sie Schmerzen ertrugen. Ich sah, wie Hoffnung aussieht und Angst, ich sah, wie sich die dunklen Linien der Verzweiflung in die menschlichen Züge eingruben, ich sah Mut und Standhaftigkeit, ich sah Vertrauen in den Augen jener leuchten, die an mich glaubten, obzwar ich wußte, dass es nur eine Illusion war; ich sah die Noblesse, mit der ein Mensch sein Todesurteil mit einem ironischen Scherzwort beantwortete, weil er zu stolz war, seine Umgebung sehen zu lassen, wie zutiefst erschrocken seine Seele war.

Alles dies war wertvolle Erfahrung für mich. Ich kenne keine bessere Schulung für einen Schriftsteller als die, einige Jahre den medizinischen Beruf auszuüben ... Ich möchte zwar nicht behaupten", so fährt Maugham fort, „dass mir die Jahre am St. Thomas's Hospital eine vollkommene Kenntnis der menschlichen Natur gegeben hätten. Ich glaube, niemand kann je hoffen, sie zu erlangen. Ich studiere die menschliche Natur, bewußt und unbewußt, seit 40 Jahren und finde noch immer unberechenbare Menschen: Leute, die ich genau zu kennen glaube, können mich plötzlich durch Handlungen überraschen, deren ich sie nie für fähig gehalten hätte, oder sie können Charakterzüge enthüllen, die ich nie bei ihnen vermutet hätte."

Maugham kommt dann auch auf die Bedeutung des „sense of humor", des Sinnes für Humor, zu sprechen: Man werde auf Leute, über die man lachen kann, nicht wütend. „You are not angry with people when you laugh at them. Humor teaches tolerance", behauptet er, „and the humorist with a smile and perhaps a sigh, is more likely to shrug his shoulders than to condemn. He does not moralize, he is content to understand, and it is true that to understand is to forgive and pity."

„Humor lehrt Toleranz, und derjenige, der Sinn für Humor hat, kann mit einem Lächeln und vielleicht mit einem Seufzer die Achseln zucken, statt zu verdammen. Wer Sinn für Humor hat, moralisiert nicht, es genügt ihm, zu verstehen, und verstehen heißt Mitleid haben und vergeben."

Als Armenarzt in den Londoner Slums hatte Maugham bereits als 24 Jähriger einen tiefen Einblick in die Abgründe und Entwürdigungen der Menschheit gewonnen, und diese Erfahrungen liegen seinem ersten, stark naturalistischen Milieuroman *Liza of Lambeth* (1898) zugrunde. Zwar stand der Roman niemals auf irgendeiner Bestsellerliste, war jedoch gerade von der französischen Kritik zur Zeit seines Erscheinens stark beachtet worden wegen seiner meisterhaften klinischen Diagnose und seiner nüchtern-distanzierten Erzählhaltung.

Während des ersten Jahrzehnts unseres Jahrhunderts lebt Maugham, der sich anfangs kümmerlich sein Brot verdienen mußte und jedes Jahr etwa einen Roman produzierte, meist in London, teils aber auch in Paris, in Italien und in Spanien. Obwohl seine Prosaschriften in jenen Jahren ihm nur gerade genug zum Leben einbringen, entdeckt er damals sein Talent für die Bühne und beginnt, Theaterstücke zu schreiben, auf die der Kritiker der *Saturday Review*, Max Beerbohm, bald aufmerksam macht.

In diesen dramatischen Arbeiten hält sich Maugham stets an die bewährte Tradition der „Comedy of Manners", d.h. an jene Form des Sittenlustspiels, das seine Dynamik aus der Beziehung des Einzelnen zur engeren oder weiteren gesellschaftlichen Umgebung der Gegenwart bezieht und damit ganz natürlich auch immer ein gesellschaftskritisches Element enthält. Hier ist es vor allem das England der oberen Mittelschicht, „the upper middle classes", das in allen denkbaren Aspekten durchleuchtet wird. Es ist dies die von Congreve, Wycherley und Sheridan begonnene Linie, auf der auch Oscar Wilde und Noël Coward stehen. Das Thema der Selbstverwirklichung, der Bestimmung des Ichs gegenüber den Ansprüchen der Konvention, wird mehr als einmal aufgegriffen und dabei dem selbständig denkenden und handelnden Menschen der Lorbeer überreicht. Besonders ansprechend geschieht dies in der Komödie *The Constant Wife* (1927), auf deutsch bekannt als *Finden Sie, dass Konstanze sich richtig verhält?*, und vor allem in *The Breadwinner* (1930), wo der von der Familie als langweiliger Geldbeschaffer betrachtete Vater unvermittelt aus dem Alltag ausbricht, mit der verwöhnten Jugend seines Hauses kühl abrechnet und unter deren beleidigter und erstaunter Bewunderung ein eigenes, für ihn sinnvolleres Leben beginnt.

Auch hier, in den Dramen, ebenso wie später in den Romanen und kurzen Erzählungen, äußert Maugham unkonventionelle Meinungen und behandelt Themen, die in der damaligen englischen Gesellschaft noch als *taboo* galten. So in *The Sacred Flame, Die Heilige Flamme*, wo das Thema der Euthanasie behandelt wird: Eine Mutter tötet ihren eigenen Sohn und empfindet keinerlei Reue über ihre Tat; in *The Unknown* gestaltet der Dichter religiöse Desillusionierung, und in *Sheppey* schließlich erzählt er die Geschichte eines christusähnlichen Mannes, der – zu gut für diese Welt – all seinen Besitz zu verschenken beginnt, bis er von seiner eigenen Familie als unzurechnungsfähig unter Kuratell gestellt wird.

Zu Beginn des Ersten Weltkriegs geht Maugham mit dem Roten Kreuz nach Frankreich, wird zunächst Ambulanzfahrer beim Britischen Expeditionskorps, ehe er wegen seiner Sprachkenntnisse als Agent vom Secret Service übernommen wird. Längere Zeit arbeitet er in dieser Eigenschaft in der Schweiz, vor allem in Genf. 1917 geht er in geheimer Mission nach Petrograd, um – wenn möglich – dazu beizutragen, den Ausbruch der Russischen Revolution zu verhindern und die Russen zur Fortsetzung des Kampfes auf Seiten der Alliierten zu bewegen. Seine Erfahrungen und Beobachtungen im englischen Geheimdienst hat er zum Teil in der unter dem Titel *Ashenden, or the British Agent* bekannten Ich-Erzählungen beschrieben.

Bevor Maugham 1916 seine Weltreisen antritt, bevor er im Rassen- und Atmosphärenproblem jenes Element findet, das seinem Denken am weitesten entgegenkommt und über das ich Ihnen heute abend einiges berichten will, hatte er sich bereits als Romancier einen Namen gemacht. Nach einigen wenig erfolgreichen Versuchen – ich erwähne nur das Frühwerk *The Magician* (1908) – ist ihm mit dem 1915 veröffentlichten Entwicklungsroman *Of Human Bondage (Der Menschen Hörigkeit)* erstmals ein großer Wurf gelungen: Dem von autobiographischen Zügen stark durchsetzten und breit angelegten Roman, der die Geschichte des klumpfüßigen Medizinstudenten Phillip Carey wiedergibt, liegt eine harte Wirklichkeit zugrunde. Diese Linie findet ihre Fortsetzung in dem 1919 erschienenen Künstlerroman *The Moon and Sixpence (Silbermond und Kupfermünze)*, dessen Held in späten Jahren dem bürgerlichen Beruf des Börsenmaklers urplötzlich den Rücken kehrt, Haus und Familie für immer verläßt und sich mit dämonischem Arbeitswillen durch alle Gefahren hindurchschleppt, bis er als Aussätziger auf einer Südseeinsel äußerlich elend zugrunde geht, aber seinen Bildern den lebendigen Geist zu geben vermag: es ist das Schicksal des Malers Paul Gauguin, das Maugham hier – ohne je seinen Namen zu nennen – gestaltet hat. Der Roman darf als klassisches Porträt eines Genius gelten, der um seiner künstlerischen Aufgabe, seiner Mission willen, alles opfert: Bequemlichkeit, Sicherheit, seinen guten Ruf, Familie, Ehre, Gesundheit, ja, man möchte fast sagen: das Leben selber. Aber für ihn selbst ist dieses der Kunst gewidmete Leben kein Mißerfolg: eine innere Notwendigkeit zwingt ihn dazu, ganz der Malerei zu leben, fern aller Zivilisation seiner europäischen Heimat.

Zwischen diesem Künstlerroman und einer weiteren Ich-Erzählung, dem Schriftstellerroman *Cakes and Ale (Derbe Kost)* (1930), verdient der in China spielende Roman *The Painted Veil (Der bunte Schleier)* vom Jahre 1925 Erwähnung. Im Mittelpunkt des Geschehens steht eine Cholera-Epidemie, die an der Frau eines englischen Arztes und Bakteriologen ein Wunder vollbringt: Der betrogene Ehemann führt nicht, wie beabsichtigt, den Tod seiner Frau herbei, indem er sie zur Strafe für ihre Untreue zwingt, ihm ins verseuchte Innere des Landes zu folgen. In Wirklichkeit geht er selbst an seiner Unfähigkeit zu vergeben zugrunde, während seine Frau durch Leideserfahrung zur Selbsterkenntnis und damit zu einem neuen Lebensinhalt gelangt.

Allein diese Leistungen berühren, trotz ihrer qualitativen Überlegenheit, beinahe als Präludien gegenüber derjenigen Kunstform, für die der Dichter am ausgesprochensten bestimmt zu sein scheint, so spät er sie auch gefunden hat: die Kurzgeschichte. Formell von der Kapazität des Dramatikers häufig ins Einaktermäßige abgebogen, spielen sie sich fast alle auf dem Hintergrund der östlichen Tropen ab, und hier verrät sich vielleicht am stärksten jene Einwirkung des französischen Realismus, vor allem Guy de Maupassants, die man Maugham gelegentlich nachgesagt hat. *The Trembling of a Leaf (Menschen der Südsee)*, die erste Sammlung seiner Short Stories, ebenso wie die zweite, *The Casuarina Tree*, sagen schon als Titel, worum es ideell und motivisch geht: Glück und Unglück des Menschen, so glaubt Maugham nach einem berühmten Wort des Franzosen Sainte-Beuve, stehen so nahe und labil beieinander, dass das Zittern eines Blattes genügt, eins ins andere umschlagen zu lassen. Der Casuarinabaum aber, dessen Wachstum den Boden des Sumpflandes zur Fruchtbarkeit veredelt, der jedoch dazu bestimmt ist, dem mächtig heranstrebenden Gewirr des Dschungels zu erliegen, flüstert nachts dem Menschen seltsame Dinge zu.

Von Menschen, Rassen, Gesellschaftsschichten in ihren eigentümlichen, mißtrauischen, herrschsüchtigen und angstvollen Beziehungen untereinander und zur nervösen Atmosphäre tropischen Schicksals berichten diese Erzählungen: vom Europäer, der eine Eingeborene zu sich nimmt und in der Lebenshaltung der dunklen Rasse allmählich erliegt; vom Emporkömmling, der mit dem gestrandeten *gentleman* zusammenstößt; vom Mischling, der beiden Rassen und keiner angehört; von der weißen Frau, die unter der Gewißheit der vorangegangenen erotischen Beziehung ihres Gatten zur anderen Rasse zusammenbricht. Feuchtfarbige Atmosphäre, endlose Dampferfahrten, exotische Mahlzeiten in abgelegenen Bungalows, mühselige Inspektionsreisen ins unbekannte Innere, bilden die Seitenkulissen zu den leidenschaftlichen Handlungen der Personen. In dieser Umgebung steht auch die Erzählung *Rain*, die in dramatisierter Form über die ganze Welt gegangen und vielleicht das bekannteste und am häufigsten verfilmte Stück Maughams geworden ist: die Geschichte jenes fanatischen Missionars, der den Bekehrungskampf bei einer Prostituierten – Miss Sadie Thompson – aufnimmt, dabei aber von ihr verführt wird und sich in seiner Verzweiflung die Kehle durchschneidet – „melodramatic", wie es die Engländer nennen, aber in der entnervenden und regengesättigten Atmosphäre des Pazifischen Ozeans irgendwie begründet.

Ich möchte den Versuch machen, Ihnen das Wesentlichste von Maugham im Fernen Osten spielenden Werken in neun Punkten auf knappem Raum wenigstens anzudeuten.

(1) In all diesen Romanen, Kurzgeschichten und Reisebüchern sowie dem Drama *East of Suez*, in denen sich Maugham mit der Welt „östlich von Suez" auseinandersetzt, hat der Dichter eine Tradition fortgesetzt, zu deren Hauptvertretern innerhalb der englischen, amerikanischen und französischen Literatur einige Ihnen bekannte Schriftsteller gehören. Ich nenne nur den Franzosen Pierre Loti, einen der führenden Darsteller des Exotismus in der Literatur; den Amerikaner Herman Melville, den Verfasser von *Moby Dick* (1851), der mehrere Jahre auf den Marquesas-Inseln sowie auf Tahiti gelebt hat, sowie seinen Landsmann Lafcadio Hearn, der Japan zu seiner Wahlheimat gemacht und auch äußerlich versucht hat, Orientale zu werden; und schließlich – im Bereiche der englisch-schottischen Literatur – Robert Louis Stevenson, Joseph Conrad, den polnischen Immigranten, der jahrelang als Offizier der britischen Handelsmarine den Fernen Osten bereist hat, sowie Rudyard Kipling, durch dessen Werk Indien und das ganze Britische Weltreich für den Engländer zu einem wirklichen Begriff geworden sind. Obwohl Maugham selber einen Einfluß der genannten Schriftsteller auf seine eigene Entwicklung

ablehnt, ist es doch keine Frage, dass er in seinen Anschauungen und in seiner Darstellung durchaus in der Tradition der englischen Kolonialschriftsteller steht, als deren letzten großen Vertreter wir Edward Morgan Forster, den Verfasser von *A Passage to India* (1924), ansehen können.

(2) Bei aller Bewunderung der östlichen Kulturen galt Maughams Anteilnahme doch in erster Linie dem Menschen, den er im Fernen Osten trifft und der ihm seine Geheimnisse offenbart. „What excited me was to meet one person after another who was new to me." Seine eigene Lebensanschauung machte als Folge dieser Begegnungen mit den Menschen des Orients einen entscheidenden Wandel durch, der sich vor allem in einer größeren Duldsamkeit manifestiert. Um seine persönliche Stellungnahme den Fragen des Lebens gegenüber auszudrücken, bedient sich Maugham zuweilen des Raisonneurs, eine Rolle, die er mit Vorliebe klugen, reifen und duldsamen Menschen überträgt, vor allem Ärzten, die dem Leben mit einem gewissen Abstand gegenüberstehen, sich aber dennoch an seinem reichen Schauspiel zu erfreuen vermögen.

(3) Trotz geringer angeborener Phantasie hat es Maugham infolge seiner scharfen Beobachtungsgabe und seines großen Interesses am Menschen niemals im Leben an Material für seine fernöstlichen Erzählungen gefehlt. Stets ist er bei seinen Charakterzeichnungen, wie er selbst zugibt, von der Beschreibung lebender Personen ausgegangen. Maugham verwahrt sich aber ausdrücklich dagegen, dass es sich bei seinen Charakteren um reine Abbilder lebender Personen handele. Nur in wenigen Fällen sind ihm die Fabeln seiner im Fernen Osten spielenden Erzählungen berichtet worden. Im Gegensatz zu einem Dichter wie Herman Melville finden wir bei ihm aber keine literarischen Quellen oder Vorbilder.

(4) Die von Maugham vorzugsweise gewählten Schauplätze sind die Samoa Inseln, Tahiti, die Hawaiischen Inseln, Borneo, der Malaiische Archipel, Burma, Siam, Französisch Indo-China und China. Im Fernen Osten und in der Südsee hat er sowohl die Schönheit der tropischen Landschaft als auch deren Gefahren gesehen und in seinem Werk dargestellt. Die exotische Umwelt bildet aber stets nur den szenischen Hintergrund. Die Beschreibung des orientalischen Milieus dient ihm lediglich zur Kennzeichnung der Atmosphäre. Niemals werden Naturschilderungen oder Straßenszenen orientalischer Städte um ihrer selbst willen gegeben.

(5) Die Beobachtung der Weißen, vor allem der Briten im Fernen Osten, war auf allen seinen Reisen das Hauptanliegen des Dichters. Maugham hat ehrlich versucht, ein realistisches Bild der englischen Regierungsvertreter, der Kolonialbeamten, Seeoffiziere, Missionare und Siedler zu geben, die er auf seinen Wanderungen getroffen hat. Immer bemüht er sich, objektiver Berichterstatter zu sein, ist es auch oft; trotzdem drängen sich, ob er will oder nicht, Sympathien und Antipathien in seine Darstellung und kann er nicht umhin, derartige Emotionen hervorzurufen. Seine Aufmerksamkeit gehört dem Leben der englischen Gesellschaft, der englischen Frau, den Klubs, wie auch den individuellen Schicksalen im Fernen Osten. Er ist besonders an den Gründen interessiert, die seine europäischen Charaktere in die exotische Welt des Fernen Ostens getrieben haben, wobei neben materiellen und gesundheitlichen Erwägungen nicht selten die Sehnsucht nach einer wahren Heimat in der noch unbekannten Ferne und die Flucht vor der westlichen Zivilisation eine Rolle spielen. Unter den von ihm beschriebenen Berufsgruppen beschäftigt sich Maugham vornehmlich mit den Kolonialbeamten, mit katholischen ebenso wie protestantischen Missionaren, daneben aber auch mit Plantagenbesitzern, Gelehrten, Künstlern, Ärzten, Seeleuten und Abenteurern. Eine Gruppe für sich bilden, wie wir gesehen hatten, die Raisonneure, die den verschiedensten Berufen angehören, im Gegensatz zu den übrigen Charakteren jedoch Maughams eigene Anschauung vertreten.

(6) Maugham ist auch am Einfluß von Umwelt und Klima auf den Europäer interessiert. Wie er einmal in einem Brief an den amerikanischen Kritiker Leslie A. Marchand schrieb: „I was very much struck by the effect of the climate and surroundings on the white people who for one reason or another had drifted there." Unter den negativen Umwelteinflüssen beobachtet er eine Beeinträchtigung des Berufsethos, eine Schwächung des sittlichen Empfindens und das Schwinden von Energie und Tatkraft. Andere Folgen des Lebens in der Einsamkeit sind die Intensivierung von Charaktereigenschaften, die in besonders starkem Maße auftreten, und die Leidenschaftlichkeit der Liebesgefühle. Doch auch günstige Einflüsse hat Maugham als Folge des langen Aufenthalts im Osten beobachtet wie die größere Toleranz in Fragen der Moral. Daneben sieht er die Gefahren der tropischen Hitze, das plötzliche Sterben oder das vorzeitige Al-

tern, und vor allem die Trunksucht, die oft zu einem frühen Ende des Menschen führt.

(7) Wiederholt hat sich Maugham mit der allgemein üblichen Einstellung des Engländers zu den Mischtypen, den Eurasiern, beschäftigt, d.h. den Vorurteilen und dem Gefühl der Überlegenheit sowie der Macht der gesellschaftlichen Konvention. Mehrmals beschreibt er das typische Mischlingsschicksal: die Zwischenstellung zwischen der weißen und der farbigen Rasse, den Kampf der beiden um die Vorherrschaft, das täuschende Erscheinungsbild der Eurasier, und deren Ausschluß aus der Gesellschaft der Europäer. Aus der Rassenmischung leitet er moralische Schwäche ab und wirft so die Frage nach dem freien Willen auf. Ausführlich behandelt er die Abneigung vor allem der Engländerinnen gegen die Eurasier sowie auch die tragische Stellung des weißen Vaters gegenüber seinen Kindern aus einer Mischehe. Obwohl alles andere als Moralist, ist Maugham durchaus Zeit seines Lebens ein Anhänger der „color bar", d.h. der Rassentrennung gewesen.

(8) Im Gegensatz zu Kiplings Werk erscheinen bei Maugham die Eingeborenen niemals in Hauptrollen. Nicht aus mangelndem Interesse, sondern wegen der Unmöglichkeit tieferen Verstehens behandelt er sie nur als Nebenfiguren. Trotzdem hat er sie scharf beobachtet und einige ihrer Merkmale beschrieben. Bei den meisten der von Maugham dargestellten Weißen, die mit Farbigen zusammenleben, fällt ihm ein völliger Mangel an Verständnis für die Psyche der „natives" auf. Daher vermögen sie auch nicht, an die Rache der verlassenen Eingeborenen zu glauben. Immer wenn Maugham Beispiele primitiven Aberglaubens anführt, tut er dies nur als unparteiischer, objektiver Beobachter und überläßt das Urteil dem Leser. Aber auch bei den Farbigen schildert Maugham Vertreter der verschiedenen Gesellschaftsschichten: gebildete Chinesen ebenso wie ganz einfache Eingeborene, und schließlich Kulis und Sklaven als Kollektivwesen. Bereits in den zwanziger Jahren hat sich Maugham mit der Frage der Verwaltung des britischen und französischen Kolonialreichs auseinandergesetzt, wobei er ein erstaunliches Verständnis für die bevorstehenden Unabhängigkeitsbestrebungen der Kolonialvölker zeigte.

(9) Auch von seiner Begegnung mit den Religionen des Fernen Ostens ist der Dichter stark beeinflußt worden. Er gibt ausführliche Darstellungen sowohl des Buddhismus als auch des Hinduismus und

glaubt vorübergehend, in der Lehre vom Karma und von der Seelenwanderung eine Antwort auf die ihn sein Leben lang quälende Fragen nach dem Sinn des Bösen in der Welt zu finden. Wie Maugham aber für seine eigene Person zugibt, kann er bei aller Bewunderung der östlichen Philosophien und Religionen keine von ihnen annehmen, er bleibt Agnostiker. Einen wirklichen Einfluß auf seine Denkweise haben die religiösen Lehren des Fernen Ostens also nicht auszuüben vermocht.

Als Maugham des Wanderns müde war, entschloß er sich 1928, endgültig Domizil aufzuschlagen. Der Dichter, der bereits als Kind und nochmals gegen Ende des Ersten Weltkriegs an Tuberkulose erkrankt war, erwarb, nicht zuletzt wegen des milden Mittelmeerklimas, die von einem katholischen Bischof im maurischen Stil erbaute Villa Mauresque auf Cap Ferrat. Erst der Ausbruch des Zweiten Weltkriegs zwang ihn zur Flucht unter Zurücklassung seines gesamten Besitzes. Im Herbst 1939 diente er als englischer Kriegskorrespondent bei der französischen Armee – seine gesammelten Artikel erschienen später unter dem Titel *France at War* – im Sommer 1940 ging er im Auftrag der britischen Regierung in die USA, wo er, anfangs offiziell im Dienste der britischen Kriegspropaganda, die nächsten sechs Jahre verbrachte. Von den in Amerika entstandenen Werken wurde der später in Hollywood verfilmte Roman *The Razor's Edge (Auf Messers Schneide)* 1944 sein größter Erfolg. Ähnlich wie Thomas Mann als „Consultant in Germanic Literature", war Maugham als „Consultant for English Literature" für die Library of Congress in Washington tätig. Und noch etwas anderes teilte er mit seinem deutschen Kollegen in der Zeit des amerikanischen Exils: im November 1948 wurde beiden die Auszeichnung zuteil, dass ihre gerade erschienenen Romane, Thomas Manns *Dokter Faustus* und Maughams *Catalina*, als „dual selection" des hochangesehenen New Yorker „Book-of-the-Month Club" weiteste Verbreitung auf dem amerikanischen Kontinent fanden.

In den fast 20 Jahren nach dem Zweiten Weltkrieg, die Maugham wieder auf seinem Besitz an der französischen Riviera verbrachte, beschäftigte er sich zum eigenen Vergnügen, wie er betonte, vor allem mit dem Schreiben von Essays und literarischer Kritik. Er verfaßte Abhandlungen über den Stil Edmund Burkes, den spanischen Maler Zurbarán, über *The Decline and Fall of the Detective Story*, über Goethes *Wahlverwandtschaften* und Kants *Kritik der reinen Vernunft*. Mehr und mehr häuften sich nun, im Alter, die Auszeichnungen, die man ihm so lange vorenthalten hatte, er wurde Ehrenritter der französischen „Légion d'Honneur", Ehrendoktor der Universitäten Toulouse und Oxford, Ehrenmitglied der American Academy of Arts and Letters in New York; die Universität Heidelberg ernannte ihn anläßlich ihrer 575. Gründungsfeier zum Ehrensenator, zum ersten Mal in der Geschichte der Universität war einem Engländer diese Anerkennung zuteil geworden. An ihrem 28. Geburtstag, dem 3. Juni 1954, empfing die englische Königin Elisabeth II. den Dichter in Privataudienz, um ihm die Insignien des „Order of the Companion of Honor" zu verleihen. Die „Royal Society of Literature", deren Vizepräsident er war, ehrte ihn zusammen mit seinem Jugendfreund Winston Churchill, E.M. Forster, John Masefield und dem Historiker G.M. Trevelyan, durch die Verleihung des Titels „Companion of Literature", eine Auszeichnung, die nur jeweils zehn Schriftsteller innehaben, „who have brought exceptional honors to English letters". Und selbst das „Vulgärpantheon" Englands, das Wachsfigurenkabinett der Madame Tussaud, beschloß, ihn in die Gruppe wächserner Geistesgrößen aufzunehmen.

Im Winter 1959/60 unternahm Maugham seine letzte große Reise in den Fernen Osten, die ihn zwar nicht mehr bis zu den Südseeinseln führte, aber dafür nach Ceylon und Singapur, nach Japan, Ankor Watt in Kambodien und nach Bangkok, wo er seinen 86. Geburtstag feierte. Als er im 88. Lebensjahr stand, lud ihn die sowjetische Regierung ein, Rußland zu besuchen, wo sich aus seinen Tantiemen eine beträchtliche Summe angesammelt hatte, die jedoch nur im Lande selbst verbraucht werden durfte. Auf Anraten seines Arztes lehnte er die Aufforderungen ab. Doch Jahr für Jahr besuchte er, nach größeren Abschiedsreisen, zum Beispiel nach Ägypten, Griechenland und der Türkei, einige Lieblingsorte in Europa, London und Paris, Rapallo und Venedig, Wien, München, Bayreuth und Bad Gastein.

Das letzte, zu seinen Lebzeiten erschienene Buch, *A Catalogue of Impressionist and Modern Pictures* nannte er nicht zu Unrecht *Purely for My Pleasure (Nur zum eigenen Vergnügen)*. Es ist ein mit kurzen Bemerkungen über seine persönlichen Beziehungen zu den Künstlern versehener, reich illustrierter Katalog seiner Gemäldesammlung, die er aus Furcht vor Diebstahl im April 1962 bei Sotheby in London zur Versteigerung gab. Schweren Herzens trennte er sich damals von diesen 32 Bildern, darunter Werken von Graham Sutherland und Marie Laurencin, Claude Monet und Henri Matisse, Picasso, Renoir, Rouault, Sisley und Utrillo. Das berühmteste war zweifellos sein besonderer Liebling, der Jahrzehnte lang sein Arbeitszimmer in der Villa Mauresque geschmückt hatte: ein Gauguin, auf Glas gemalt, den er sich 1916 für 400 Franken aus Tahiti mitgebracht hatte. „Even if I were going out to dinner", schreibt Maugham in seinem kurzen Vorwort, „I could not be sure that a thief would not take the opportunity to steal one or two of my pictures. For many years they had given me great pleasure; now they were an anxiety. I decided to sell them. I hope that you will get as much pleasure out of such as you buy tonight as I have got out of them in the past." Es ist bezeichnend für Somerset Maugham, dass er den Erlös von über 5 Millionen Pfund dem „Royal Literary Fund" zur Unterstützung armer englischer Schriftsteller gestiftet hat.

In seinem Buch *Rückblick auf mein Leben (The Summing Up)* zitiert Maugham am Schlusse einen Ausspruch des Spaniers Fray Luis de Leon, der auch für ihn selber charakteristisch ist und mit dem ich meine Ausführungen heute abend beschließen will: „The beauty of life is nothing but this: that each should act in conformity with his nature and his business".

Aus dem Briefwechsel mit Somerset Maugham

Bis zum Januar 1941 hatte ich den Namen des englischen Schriftstellers Somerset Maugham niemals gehört. In einer Seminarübung für angehende Anglisten an der Universität Greifswald erwähnte der Inhaber des Lehrstuhls, Professor Reinhard Haferkorn, einmal beiläufig den Namen dieses Autors, der zwar eine viele Millionen zählende weltweite Leserschaft hatte, jedoch von der seriösen Kritik gerade seines eigenen Landes lange Zeit ungerecht behandelt oder sogar ignoriert worden war. Sähe man einmal von seinem großen Entwicklungsroman *Of Human Bondage* (*Von der Menschen Hörigkeit*, 1915 ab, den der Kritiker Theodore Dreiser als Meisterwerk dieser Gattung bezeichnet hatte, so seien seine in der Südsee oder in Ostasien spielenden Werke, vor allem seine „Short Stories" zweifellos das Beste, was es auf dem Gebiet der englischen Kolonialliteratur überhaupt gäbe. Eine Dissertation über das Thema „Somerset Maugham und der Ferne Osten" sei daher längst überfällig. Ob sich wohl einer der Teilnehmer für dieses Desideratum interessieren würde? Sicher eine rhetorische Frage, da wir uns alle noch als Anfänger fühlten und keiner sich mit dem Thema einer späteren Dissertation beschäftigte. Ich hatte aufmerksam zugehört, hatte jedoch vorerst keine Möglichkeit, Maughams Werke auch nur leihweise zu bekommen. Wegen seiner Tätigkeit als Agent im britischen Secret Service im Ersten Weltkrieg stand Maughams Name auf der vom Propagandaminister Dr. Goebbels herausgegebenen Schwarzen Liste der verbotenen Bücher.

Als ich im akademischen Jahr 1941/42 an der Friedrich-Wilhelms-Universität in Berlin studierte, ahnte ich nicht, dass einer meiner dortigen Lehrer, Helmut Papajewski, gerade eine Monographie über den englischen Autor vorbereitete, die allerdings erst sieben Jahre nach Kriegsende erschien.[1] Doch ein glücklicher Zufall wollte es, dass eine in USA gebürtige ältere Nachbarin eine amerikanische Zeitschrift, die von Benjamin Franklin begründete *Saturday Evening Post* abonnierte. In den April- und Mai-Nummern 1942, die ich bei ihr ausleihen durfte, fand ich einen Vorabdruck aus Maughams nächstem Buch, *Strictly Personal*[2], einem Bericht über seine Erlebnisse und Erfahrungen während der Flucht aus Südfrankreich zu Beginn des Zweiten Weltkriegs. Durch diese mich fesselnden Artikel erwachte in mir die Neugier auf die Lektüre weiterer Werke dieses Schriftstellers. Trotz der schwierigen Postverhältnisse im Nachkriegs-Deutschland konnte ich im Sommer 1946 brieflichen Kontakt mit dem Autor aufnehmen, der nach sechsjähriger Abwesenheit kurz zuvor in seine Villa Mauresque an der Französischen Riviera zurückgekehrt war. In einem meiner ersten Briefe schickte ich ihm eine unbedeutende Auftragsarbeit mit einem Artikel aus der Zeitschrift *Das Weltbild*[3] sowie eine Bildermappe mit Stichen von Heidelberg, wo Maugham mehr als fünfzig Jahre zuvor eine unbeschwert-glückliche Studienzeit zugebracht und die neugewonnene Freiheit nach der Schulzeit in Canterbury in vollen Zügen genossen hatte. Offenbar war es mir gelungen, ihm mit dieser Sendung eine kleine Freude zu bereiten, zumal sie aus der unzerstörten Stadt am Neckar, meinem damaligen Wohnsitz, zu ihm kam. Persönlich dankte er mir für den anspruchslosen kleinen Artikel „and the charming book of Heidelberg pictures. They made me feel very sentimental."

Kurz vor Beginn meiner Studienzeit in Genf[4] fragte ich Maugham im Interesse meiner geplanten Dissertation nach seinen Reisen in den Fernen Osten, und in seinem Brief vom 16. April 1947 gab er mir bereitwillig die gewünschte Auskunft:

> „It is very difficult for me to give you the information you seek because I never kept a diary of my journeys, and so my dates are very vague. The following is the best I can do. I spent the winter of 1916–17 in Oceania and visited the Hawaian Islands, the Samoan Group and Tahiti. I was there altogether about six months. In 1920 I went to China and spent several months there. The results were my book *On A Chinese Screen*, my novel *The Painted Veil* and a play called *East Of Suez*. In 1921 I think I went to the Federated Malay States, Indo-China and again to China. I believe it was in the year 1922, that I went to Australia and visited a number of islands in the Malay Archipelago. It was on that journey that I spent three months in Java. I think it must have been the following year that I went again to the Malay States and Borneo, and took a journey through the Shan States ending up with Siam, from where I went to Ankor. I do not quite know what year that brings me up to but the year after that I think I must have gone to the West Indies and to various Central and South American States. After that I made no more long journeys until 1937, when I went to India for the winter. This is the best information I can give you. On all my journeys I spent about five or six months because I felt that I could not absorb after that period. I am reminded in writing this that I spent a winter in California before I went to Australia. On that occasion I was away from Europe fifteen months".

In meinen ersten Amerikajahren hatte ich mehr als einmal Gelegenheit, Maugham während seiner USA-Reisen in seiner Suite im Plaza Hotel in New York zu begegnen und nicht nur berufliche, sondern auch persönliche Fragen mit ihm besprechen zu können. Durch ein Empfehlungsschreiben an einen alten Bekannten, John Marshall, Associate Director der Rockefeller Foundation, vom 18. Januar 1949 versuchte er, meine Bewerbung um ein Stipendium der Columbia University zu unterstützen:

> „I venture to write to you to recommend Mr. Klaus Jonas/ who desires to obtain a tuition grant from the Rockefeller Foundation/ which will enable him to take his degree as Master of Arts in the English/ Department of Columbia University with the idea after this of securing/ a situation as information officer and librarian of the U.S. Information/ Service in Zurich, Switzerland, which, I understand, is to be established/ in the course of this year/. From personal acquaintance and a somewhat lengthy period of/ correspondence I have formed a high opinion of his intelligence and/ industry, so that I have little doubt that he would be in every way/ a worthy recipient of the grant for which he is applying."

Nach einem längeren Gespräch und gründlicher Überprüfung meiner „credentials" bewarb ich mich auf Anraten von Mr. Marshall um einen Lehrposten in einer der bekannten „Ivy League Schools", dem Mount Holyoke College in Massachusetts.[5] In der College-Bibliothek verbrachte ich viele Stunden zwecks Arbeit an der Dissertation. Als eine Art „Nebenprodukt"[6] erschien im Sommer 1950 mein erster schmaler Band über den Schriftsteller. Am 25. Juli bedankte sich zunächst Maughams Sekretär Alan Searle für sein Exemplar dieses Nachschlagewerks:

> „It is going to be a very useful book to me in my work, and will save me hours of searching. I am grateful to you. I hope so much that you will have success with it. I shall certainly advise all the many people who write to me for information to consult it."

Auch Maugham selbst dankte noch am selben Tag:

> „I had only had time to glance through it but my impression is very favorable. It is clear that you have taken a great deal of trouble, and I sincerely hope it will prove to have been worth your while."

Von Anfang an nahm Maugham am Aufbau unserer Existenz in der Neuen Welt regen Anteil und verfolgte unsere berufliche Laufbahn mit nie nachlassendem Interesse.

> „I am very glad to think that you are now comfortably settled and I hope on the way to academic success,"

schrieb er mir am 26. August 1950. Damals plante ich, eine Sammlung ausgewählter Kritiken, positiver ebenso wie negativer, über sein Lebenswerk herauszubringen. Als ich ihn darüber informierte, zeigte er sogleich Interesse an meinem Plan:

> „With regard to the anthology your proposed to call *The Stature of Somerset Maugham*, of course I cannot fail to be interested in the idea, and can only hope that you will not find the time you must inevitably spend on it entirely wasted."

Im ersten meiner fünf Jahre an der Rutgers University in New Jersey bereitete ich zu Ehren des Autors in der Universitätsbibliothek eine Ausstellung mit Originalmanuskripten, Briefen, Erst- und Widmungsexemplaren seiner Werke sowie Übersetzungen in fremde Sprachen vor. Leihgaben kamen aus Harvard und Yale, der New York Public Library sowie der Library of Congress. Den Einführungsvortrag bei der Eröffnung am 5. Februar 1951 hielt der beste Maugham-Kenner in Amerika, der Kritiker Richard A. Cordell.

Inzwischen machte die Arbeit an der Dissertation gute Fortschritte. Wiederholt betonte Maugham, dass er gern bereit sei, Fragen zu beantworten. Typisch für seine präzisen Antworten ist die folgende:

> „Why I have never tried to depict the natives in the Far East was that I did not believe any European could get into the inside of them, and I felt that all the depictions that had been made of either Chinese, Indians or Malayas were merely superficial impressions combined with a lot of conventional prejudices. It is very nearly impossible for an English author to create a French character so that a French reader would accept him as real. How much more difficult then would it be for an English writer to create a Chinese the Chinese would accept as plausible."

Als ich im Herbst 1951 bei Maugham anfragte, ob er bereit und gewillt wäre, meine in deutscher Sprache geschriebene Dissertation zu lesen, antwortete er aus dem Dorchester Hotel in London:

> „Of course I will read your dissertation if you wish me to, though I am afraid I shall not be able to make any comments that would be useful to you. But in any case you don't need my approval to publish it because whatever you say will be your honest opinion, and I can ask for nothing else."

Das Manuskript meiner Arbeit an der Anthologie verlegerisch in England oder Amerika unterzubringen, bereitete mir anfangs Schwierigkeiten, über die ich den Autor ganz offen informierte. Ich schrieb ihm auch, dass ich bereit wäre, den Druck der geplanten Arbeit über ihn notfalls selbst zu finanzieren, aber da gab er mir am 16. Dezember 1952 einen wohlgemeinten Rat:

> „I am sorry that you have had so much trouble over your anthology. I am afraid that you must resign yourself to the fact that if no publisher is prepared to publish it at his own expense there is no demand for such a book. I have had a good deal of experience with publishers, and I am convinced that it is never worth while for an author to publish a book at his own expense."

Trotz der anfänglichen Enttäuschung wegen der negativen Antworten verschiedener Verleger gab ich meinen Plan nicht auf und war froh, dem Autor rechtzeitig zu seinem 80. Geburtstag den Band schicken zu können.

Im Sommer 1953 hatte ich Maugham meinen ersten ihn betreffenden Artikel aus einer deutschen Literaturzeitschrift geschickt. Ich wusste, dass er mühelos Deutsch lesen konnte. Bereits am 14. Juni dankte er mir für die Zusendung meiner Würdigung, die er mit Interesse gelesen habe:

> „I could not be more flattered."[7]

Wenn er auch immer wieder betonte, niemals etwas ihn Betreffendes zu lesen, so machte er doch gelegentlich Ausnahmen, ja einmal bemühte er sich sogar selbst um die Verbreitung einer Monographie über sein Werk. So hatte ich ihm ein Exemplar der Arbeit von Helmut Papajewski zukommen lassen, von der er anfangs ungewöhnlich angetan, später jedoch recht enttäuscht war. Im selben Brief vom 14. Juli heißt es:

> „I am reading it now, and if I had his address I should like to write to him when I have finished it. He seems to have taken an infinite amount of trouble. My English publisher has just arrived here and I am going to talk to him about the possibility of having it translated into English. Even though I have thus far only read part of it, I can tell that no book so thorough and so discerning has ever been written about my works."

Bereits vor Jahren hatte Maugham mir geschrieben, dass er aller Voraussicht nach nicht noch einmal im Leben nach Amerika kommen würde. Dennoch bemühte ich mich weiterhin um eine akademische Auszeichnung des Autors. Auch zu diesem Problem nahm er Stellung in seinem Brief vom 5. September 1953:

> „I am deeply obliged to you for the efforts you have been taking to get Rutgers University to grant me an honorary degree. I must, however, with regret, ask you to have the matter stopped. You see, no degrees appear to be granted in absentia, and my great age, and the frail health that accompanies it, make it impossible for me to make the exhaustive journey to the United States. Exhaustive not so much on account of the journey as on the inevitable activities which are forced upon me. I have had to refuse, on this account, two honorary degrees which very distinguished universities desired to confer on me."

Im Januar 1954 konnte Maugham bei guter Gesundheit seinen 80. Geburtstag begehen, überwältigt von Hunderten von Glückwünschen und Geschenken aus aller Welt. Unter diesen befand sich auch unsere Anthologie der Kritik, *The Maugham Enigma,*[8] mit Beiträgen führender Schriftsteller wie Paul Dottin, Graham Greene, Ludwig Lewisohn, Leslie A. Marchand, Charles Morgan and Mark Van Doren.

> „It looks a very handsome volume, and I realize it must have cost you a lot of trouble to get together. I will not pretend that I have read it, for I have a most violent disinclination to read anything that is written about me."

Alan Searle dagegen hat den Band gelesen und bedankte sich mit den Worten:

> „I am delighted to have it, and have, of course, read it with great interest. One of these days, when we meet, we really must get down to discussing Mr. Maugham. None of these people begin to know the man really. He is much more of an enigma than anyone realises. As I read their views and opinions, I fail to recognize the man with whom I have lived on the terms of closest intimacy for twenty-five years."

Der nächste längere Brief von Maugham vom 14. Mai 1956 erschien zuerst als Vorwort zu meiner Publikation *The Gentleman from Cap Ferrat*[9] und ist in diesem Band wieder abgedruckt.

Zur selben Zeit erschien in einem literaturwissenschaftlichen Jahrbuch in Deutschland mein Beitrag über „Maugham Collections in America."[10] Offenbar hat sich der Autor auch über diesen Artikel gefreut, wie man seinem Brief vom 29. August 1956 entnehmen kann:

> „I am properly impressed by the immense amount of work you have put into these pages. No one can be more conscious than I am that in a very few years after my death I may be entirely forgotten, and then all these collections of manuscripts, typescripts and letters will be merely waste paper."

Er konnte nicht wissen, dass das genaue Gegenteil der Fall sein würde.

Im selben Brief berichtet Maugham auch über sein Privatleben und die gelegentlich anstrengenden Besucher oder Logiergäste, die zu ihm kommen und seine Gastfreundschaft in Anspruch nehmen:

> „Friends and family and visitors come for a change of air or a holiday and naturally want to be entertained. They do not realise that this is my working place and that they disrupt the routine of my life. They do not know that a writer does not only work when he is at his desk, he writes all day long even though he does not put pen on paper. They leave me exhausted."

Regelmäßig berichtete Alan Searle über die gemeinsamen Reisen oder Kuraufenthalte. Am 19. Mai 1958 schrieb er aus dem Hotel Trois Couronnes in Vevey:

> „We came here to see Professor Niehans,[11] and I have been rejuvenated. It was very painful, and very expensive, but I hope it will be successful."

Und am 20. Juni, nach seiner Rückkehr an die Riviera, schrieb er recht zufrieden nach Beendigung der Kur:

> „I have returned from the hands of Professor Niehans. I am so full of lamb and young bull, that when I get excited, I don't know whether to baa or bellow."

Am 25. Januar 1959 vollendete Maugham sein 85. Lebensjahr in seiner Villa Mauresque. Unter den Glückwünschen und Geschenken waren auch zwei Bücher, die seine besondere Aufmerksamkeit fanden: Das in New York erschienene Werk eines alten Bekannten, eines amerikanischen Schriftstellers,[12] eine ohne seine Einwilligung und gegen seinen Wunsch verfasste biographische Studie, sowie meine seit langem vorbereitete Anthologie der Kritik, *The World of Somerset Maugham*.[13] Zu beiden Werken nahm er in seinem Brief an mich vom 22. Januar Stellung:

> „My dear Klaus,
> Alan and I got back from Italy two days ago and I found your book waiting for me. It comes as a pleasant antidote to Karl Pfeiffer's work (I have forgotten the name already). I have a great disinclination to read what is written about me, but in this case, since my friends were so indignant I thought I better read his book and see what it is all about. It is vulgar and very inaccurate, somehow spiteful, but otherwise harmless enough. It is also careless. He reports that I had an interview with Gandhi ignorant of the fact that Gandhi died before I ever went to India. He sneers because the men servants at table wear liveries, ignorant of the meaning of the word livery. As a fact they have

> white ducks which is the usual wear of everyone in summer. These are only two of the many mistakes he has made. But what do they matter? The only thing that puzzles me is why, considering that I have always been kind to him and that he enjoyed my hospitality (not so much as he proclaimed, however) he should apparently have always regarded me with ill will. It is not very pretty, though perhaps human, to bite the hand that feeds you.
> Shall we see you both here in the summer? Yours always, Wm."

Und dann folgt noch ein Wort der Anerkennung von *The World of Somerset Maugham*, das mich natürlich besonders gefreut hat:

> „You know that I don't read things about myself, but I know that I have reason to be grateful to you for the tribute you have edited."

Die rechtzeitig zu seinem Geburtstag erschienene Anthologie mit Maughams Vorwort enthielt außer einem Kapitel aus meiner Dissertation Essays bekannter Schriftsteller wie St. John Ervine, Frank Swinnerton und Glenway Wescott. Auch Alan Searle bedankte sich am 24. Januar für sein Exemplar:

> „I am really delighted with it. I think it is quite splendid. It had a very good notice in the ‚Daily Telegraph' from Lord Birkenhead. Mr. Maugham was very much touched and pleased by the book, and tears were very near."

Immer wieder hatten Maugham und Alan Searle den Wunsch, unsere Sammlung durch ihre zahlreichen Geschenke zu vervollständigen:

> „I have been thinking of the Maugham Centre. I have a pretty good collection of Maughamiana, and all the first editions. Would you like me to leave them to the Center?"[14]

Selbst als 85-Jähriger hatte Maugham die Vitalität und „intellectual curiosity", noch ein letztes Mal im Leben eine mehrmonatige Reise in den Fernen Osten anzutreten. Ich hatte ihm von dem japanischen Übersetzer von *The World of Somerset Maugham*, einem Anglistik-Professor namens Mutsuo Tanaka in Tokio berichtet, dem es eine Ehre und Freude sein würde, Maugham und Alan Searle als „Cicerone" dienen zu dürfen. Tanaka hatte mich um meine Vermittlung gebeten. Im letzten Absatz seines Briefes an mich vom 19. Juni 1959 aus dem Grand Hôtel de l'Europe in Bad Gastein sprach Maugham von seiner Vorfreude auf die Begegnung mit seinem großen Verehrer in Japan:

> „I was very much pleased to get your letter, but disappointed that you and Doris[15] are not coming to Europe this summer. Don't leave it too long before you come again. Alan and I have been taking the cure here; it is very exhaust-

> ing, but we are promised that in four or five weeks we shall benefit by it. Anyhow Toscanini came here every year and they kept him alive till he was over ninety. I have been trying to recover something of the German I used to speak unto over half a century ago, but it is being difficult since everyone here speaks English and wants to practice it on me. From here we go to Vienna for a week and then on to Venice for another week, after which the car meets us and we drive home. We have been away for quite a long time and I am eager to get back to my garden, my books and the odds and ends I am amusing myself by writing."

Zu meiner Freude wollte Maugham den Übersetzer meines Buches in Tokio kennenlernen:

> „Thank you for telling me about Professor Mutsuo Tanaka. I am sure I shall like to meet him. You see, it is more than thirty years since I was in Japan and I shall be lost if I don't find someone who can help me to know what I should see and how best to see it. There is an English writer, Francis King, a good writer, who is living in Tokyo now and I am sure he will do what he can to make my visit pleasant."

Am 25. November 1959 berichtet Alan Searle aus dem Mikyako Hotel in Tokio über ihre bisherige Reise in den Fernen Osten:

> „Here we are, in Japan, and Mr. Maugham is enjoying a very great triumph indeed. On the voyage out we stopped at Aden, Bombay, Colombo, Singapore, Manila, Hong Kong, and Kobe, and at each place, the Press and photographers poured on board, and when finally we reached Yokohama, they came aboard by the hundreds, and when we disembarked there was a crowd of several thousand people waiting to greet him. Our stay in Tokyo was one long success, and at the exhibition of Mr. Maugham's books etc. three hundred people were invited, and over five thousand turned up! And there were great crowds in the streets outside.
> I am loving Japan. It is a beautiful country and most exciting. They are all gerontophiles, too, so I am having a lovely time, it hasn't been so good for me since I was twelve."

Schon lange hatte ich darüber nachgedacht, ob ich nach dem gescheitertem Versuch, Maugham zu einem amerikanischen Ehrendoktor zu verhelfen, es nicht einmal mit seiner deutschen Alma mater versuchen sollte. So wies ich den Rektor der Universität Heidelberg auf die Stellung des Autors in der englischen Gegenwartsliteratur hin und schlug ihm vor, dem 87-jährigen Schriftsteller die Würde eines Ehrendoktors zu verleihen.

Und diesmal gelang es tatsächlich. Wie mir Maugham am 11. April 1961 schrieb:

> „I need not tell you how pleased I am and how grateful I am to you for having worked it. You must have certain charming ways of persuasion. Now I must ask you for information on an important matter. Alfred Ayer, the philosopher, tells me I should wear full evening dress with my orders. Is that right or shall I wear an ordinary black suit? If you can tell me I shall be much obliged."

Nach der Verleihung der Würde eines Ehrensenators am 31. Mai[16] zeigte sich auch Alan Searle sehr angetan von dem ganzen Unternehmen:

> „They really made me proud. Mr. Maugham got an enormous reception from the students. I was staggered by it; and the authorities made him an honorary Senator – the first Englishman in the history of the University."

Da Maugham bisher nur den ins Englische übersetzten Teil meiner deutsch verfassten Dissertation kannte, fragte ich bei ihm an, ob er sich dafür interessieren würde, die ganze Arbeit einmal anzusehen. Mit seiner Einwilligung schickte ich also im Herbst 1961 ein Exemplar der Dissertation nach Cap Ferrat, für das er sich am 28. Dezember bedankte:

> „I got back here on Christmas Eve, and since then, have been reading your book. I finished it yesterday. As you may imagine, I found it of great interest, and I must confess that you have told me certain things about myself that I had never quite realised. I am deeply impressed by the thoroughness with which you have treated your subject, and the amount of work you must have had to do in consequence. Of course I cannot pretend to be a judge of German style, but it seems to me that you have written in a very easy, simple manner, and that, as you know, is a form of writing I am very much in favor of."

Obwohl ich nicht wusste, ob und wie weit sich Maugham für deutsche Geschichte interessierte, schickte ich ihm auf gut Glück auch ein Exemplar meines nächsten Buches, der Biographie des letzten Kronprinzen Wilhelm.[17] Natürlich kannte Maugham ihn nicht persönlich, war jedoch mit dessen jüngstem, in England mit einer Guinness-Erbin verheirateten, Sohn Frederick, Prince of Prussia, gut bekannt. Und am 22. August 1962 schrieb er mir darüber:

> „I waited to thank you for sending me your book till I had read it. I finished reading it this afternoon and found it most interesting. I was properly im-

pressed by the bibliography – good heavens, what an amount of work you must have done! Your portrait of the Crown Prince is fascinating. Though he was by way of being a mess his end is moving."

In jedem meiner Geburtstagsbriefe erzählte ich Maugham auch von unseren Reiseplänen, für die er sich besonders zu interessieren schien. Am 13. Januar 1963 dankte er uns mit folgenden Worten:

„Dear Klaus, Thank you for your charming letter and all the nice things you say, and for your good wishes. It was extremely kind of you to write to me: I was touched and much pleased. I hope that you and Doris will be coming to Europe this summer and that we shall all meet again. I think of you often and with much affection. Yours always, Wm."

In seinen letzten Lebensjahren trennte sich Maugham nicht nur von einem Großteil seiner Sammlung moderner Kunst, sondern auch von seiner Bibliothek. Bei jedem unserer Besuche durften wir uns eine Reihe unserer Sammlung noch fehlender Bücher aussuchen.

„Thank you for your lovely letter,"

schrieb Alan Searle am 21. Juli 1963 über die zurückgelassenen Exemplare, die uns noch nicht erreicht hatten:

„I cannot tell you what it means to me – you and Doris are wonderful friends, and I wish you knew how much I love you. Some of the books are on the way – any that remain, you must pick out on your next visit."

Ein anderes wiederholt mit Maugham und Alan Searle besprochenes Thema war der einstige Schüler des Lübecker Katharineums, der berühmte Bildhauer Fritz Behn, zu dem Maugham eine besondere Sympathie empfand. Er hatte vor Jahren eine Büste von Maugham aus Terracotta angefertigt, die eines Tages in unsere Sammlung gelangen sollte. Am 15. November 1963 äußerte sich Alan Searle auch zu diesem Thema:

„I love Munich, and could be very happy here. I attended the Oktoberfest and got uproariously drunk. We did not see Professor Behn this time. The bust we have here belongs to me. I will give it to you eventually."[18]

Meine Erinnerungen gehen zurück an die ersten Begegnungen in New York in den 40er Jahren, an Spaziergänge mit Maugham und Alan Searle durch die Altstadt von Villefranche, an gemeinsame Mahlzeiten in seinem Stammlokal, Le Corsaire, bei dem mehrere Fotos entstanden, oder seinen Besuch in unserem Hotel in Beaulieu-sur-mer. Dankbar erinnere ich mich auch des

Briefwechsels mit Maughams ältestem Freund, Bertram Alanson, zu dem ich in meinen ersten Jahren in Amerika guten Kontakt hatte. Jahrzehnte hindurch war er, der Präsident der San Francisco Stock Exchange, eine Art finanzieller Berater Maughams gewesen. Einmal fragte ich den Autor nach seiner ersten Begegnung mit diesem Bewunderer seines literarischen Werkes, und am 29. August 1956 schrieb er mir über den Anfang ihrer Freundschaft:

> „It was in 1916. I was in a ship sailing from Los Angeles to Honolulu and he was a fellow passenger. I went on to Samoa and on my return to America saw him in San Francisco on landing. So began a friendship which has lasted for forty years. I owe him a very great deal. I gave him the manuscript of *The Trembling of a Leaf* on his first visit to me here. No one could have been a more devoted, generous, considerate friend than dear Bert."

Vom 25. Mai bis zum 1. August 1958 zeigte die Stanford University in Kalifornien „A Comprehensive Exhibition of the Writings of W. Somerset Maugham." Unter den Leihgebern waren Familienmitglieder, Freunde wie Bertram Alanson und Sir Gerald Kelly, aber auch Bibliotheken wie die Pierpont Morgan Library, die Princeton University Library, die United States Library of Congress und die Yale University Library. Das Widmungsexemplar dieses Katalogs enthält die folgende Eintragung:

> „This exhibition was largely arranged by an old friend of mine, Bertram Alanson. He was dying and asked his doctors to keep him alive till May 25th so that he could visit it. He died on that day before he could see it.
>
> W. Somerset Maugham
> for Klaus Jonas"

> This exhibition was largely arranged by an old friend of mine Bertram Alanson. He was dying + asked his doctors to keep him alive till May 25ᵗʰ so that he could visit it. He died on that day before he could see it.
>
> W. Somerset Maugham
>
> for Claus Jonas.

Zum letzten Mal im Leben besuchte ich beide, Maugham und Alan, am 29. September 1964. Zwar schien er mir sichtlich gealtert, aber geistig unverändert und nach wie vor am Schicksal seiner Freunde interessiert. Niemals werde ich seine Hilfsbereitschaft, seine Gastfreundschaft und die vielfältige Förderung meiner Projekte während der vergangenen zwei Jahrzehnte vergessen. Seine zahlreichen Geschenke befinden sich in der Sammlung Jonas im Humanities Research Center der University of Texas, wo sie für Forschungszwecke allen Interessenten zur Verfügung stehen.

Anmerkungen:
1 Helmut Papajewski:
 Die Welt-, Lebens- und Kunstanschauung William Somerset Maughams. Köln, 1952.
2 W. Somerset Maugham:
 The Death of France. In: *Saturday Evening Post*, 22. März 1941
 Little Things of No Consequence. In: *Saturday Evening Post*, 29. März 1941
 We have been betrayed. In: *Saturday Evening Post*, 5. April 1941
 Escape to America. In: *Saturday Evening Post*, 12. April 1941
 Diese vier Artikel erschienen in Buchform unter dem Titel *Strictly Personal* (New York, 1941; London, 1942)
3 Klaus W. Jonas:
 W. Somerset Maugham schreibt seinen letzten Roman. In: *Das Weltbild*, Jg. 2, Heft 10 (2. Juniheft 1947). [*Catalina*]
4 Wegen der Schwierigkeiten, im Nachkriegs-Deutschland an Maughams Werke zu gelangen, versuchte ich 1946 mit allen Mitteln, vom Alliierten Kontrollrat in Berlin ein Ausreise-Permit für eine Studienreise in die Schweiz zu bekommen. In diesem Zusammenhang erwies sich das Empfehlungsschreiben des Lehrstuhlinhabers für Anglistik der Universität Würzburg, Professor J.P. Leidig vom 16. Juni 1946 als besonders nützlich:

 Würzburg, 16.6.46
 „This is to certify that Herr Klaus Jonas is engaged on a dissertation dealing with the literary work of Mr. Somerset Maugham. He is up against the great difficulty of securing the necessary books. This difficulty is almost insurmountable in view of the many bombed-out and displaced libraries as well as the prevailing disruption of communications in Germany.

 I therefore warmly support his application for a permit to go to Geneva. Herr Jonas has always shown himself to be a staunch opponent of the Nazi régime and has managed to keep up friendly relations with many people abroad, even when such relations were viewed with suspicion by the Nazi authorities. Hence there should be no objection to his going abroad from the political point of view. And the projected stay in Geneva would provide him with the very opportunity he so badly needs to get on and finish the work on which he had already spent so much time and labor."

5 Am 10. Mai 1949 schrieb mir John Marshall, den ich über mein erstes Lehramt in Amerika informiert hatte: „I appreciate your kindness in writing to tell me that you had been appointed as an Assistant in the Department of German at Mount Holyoke College. This is indeed good news – and, as you will agree, a most interesting example of the utility of the UNESCO Handbook without which neither of us would have known of this possibility."
6 Bei dem „Nebenprodukt", entstanden während der Ausarbeitung der Dissertation, handelt es sich um den Band *A Bibliography of the Writings of W. Somerset Maugham* (South Hadley, Massachusetts, 1950).

7 Klaus W. Jonas: W. Somerset Maugham. In: *Archiv für das Studium der Neueren Sprachen und Literaturen*, Bd. 189, Jg. 104, Nr. 4 (April 1953), S. 326–330. Englischer Text in: *Books Abroad*, Jg. 33, Nr. 1 (Winter 1958), S. 20–24.
8 Klaus W. Jonas: *The Maugham Enigma*. An Anthology (London, New York, 1954).
9 Zuerst veröffentlicht als Vorwort zu dem Band von Klaus W. Jonas, *The Gentleman from Cap Ferrat* (New Haven, Connecticut, 1956).
   Am 22. Januar 1957 schrieb ein Freund und Kollege von Somerset Maugham, der amerikanische Schriftsteller Carl Van Vechten, über diesen Band: „The Gentleman from Cap Ferrat arrived yesterday afternoon. I read it immediately and found it utterly charming. Willie should be delighted with it. One of the principal virtues is that it is not TOO long. On the whole, I think it is your masterpiece to date!"
10 Klaus W. Jonas: W. Somerset Maugham Collections in America. In: *Jahrbuch für Amerikastudien*, Bd. 3 (1958), S. 205–213.
11 Professor Paul Niehans hatte zeitweise große Erfolge in seiner exklusiven Privatklinik in Vevey am Genfer See. Nachdem Maugham und Alan Searle von verschiedenen Seiten gehört hatten, dass sich einige ihrer Bekannten der von Niehans entwickelten Frischzellenkur unterzogen hatten, beschlossen auch sie, sich in der Niehans-Klinik behandeln zu lassen.
12 Der Anglist an der New York Universitiy Karl G. Pfeiffer war bereits einmal im Mai 1945 mit einem längeren Portrait „Maugham – as I Know Him" in der amerikanischen Zeitschrift *Redbook Magazine* hervorgetreten. Statt wie geplant eine Biographie des englischen Autors zu verfassen, veröffentlichte er den Band *W. Somerset Maugham: A Candid Portrait* (New York, 1959).
13 Klaus W. Jonas: *The World of Somerset Maugham*. An Anthology (London, New York 1949). Ins Japanische übersetzt von Mutsuo Tanaka (Tokio, 1959). Reprint Edition: Westport, Connecticut, 1972.
   Am 14. April 1959 schrieb der amerikanische Schriftsteller Carl Van Vechten: „At last I have read *The World of Somerset Maugham* from cover to cover and I think it is only fair to tell you that I believe it is, on the whole, the best picture of Maugham that has yet appeared. The various chapters compliment and supplement each other and there is very little overlapping. I think you are to be warmly congratulated for the work you have done on this man. Of course Maugham says he doesn't like books about himself and never reads them, but if he DID read this one, I believe he might like it. You have been fair and quoted the bad as well as the good."
14 Das vom Verfasser dieses Bandes begründete Center of Maugham Studies in New Haven, Connecticut, sollte als eine Art „clearing house of information about Somerset Maugham" dienen. Die mit Hilfe von Maugham und Alan Searle aufgebaute Sammlung gelangte 1966 in eine der größten amerikanischen „Rare Book Libraries", das von Thomas F. Staley geleitete Harry Ransom Humanities

Research Center der University of Texas in Austin. Die dortige Sammlung von Maughams Manuskripten gehört zusammen mit Stanford University und Yale zu den umfassendsten auf dem amerikanischen Kontinent. Nach der Yale University Library besitzt Texas heute auch eine der wichtigsten Thomas Mann Sammlungen in Amerika im Alfred A. Knopf Room, in dem sich der Nachlass von Manns amerikanischen Verleger und Freund befindet. Vgl. Klaus W. Jonas: The Center of Maugham Studies. In: *Pitt* (Universitiy of Pittsburgh), Heft 64 (Herbst 1958), S. 16–18.

15 Doris: Gemeint ist die Literaturwissenschaftlerin Ilsedore B. Jonas, die bei sämtlichen Begegnungen mit Somerset Maugham und Alan Searle (bis auf September 1964) anwesend war. Beim ersten Besuch am 29. Juli 1955 widmete der Autor ihr ein Exemplar seines Buches *Don Fernando*: „For /Mrs. Klaus Jonas/ to read when she goes to Spain."

16 Die Auszeichnung durch die Universität Heidelberg am 31. Mai 1961 bedeutete für Maugham die Erfüllung eines großen Wunsches. Voller berechtigtem Stolz zeigte er ausgewählten Freunden die ihm verliehene Goldmedaille.

Ruprecht-Karl-Universität Heidelberg
Rektorat des Professors Dr. Gottfried Köthe
Der Senat der Universität Heidelberg
verleiht
Mr. William Somerset Maugham
die Würde eines
Ehrensenators

Die Universität ehrt in ihm einen großen englischen Romancier,
Dramatiker und Essayisten, dessen Werk durch die unbestechliche Darstellung
menschlicher Charaktere auch in Deutschland starken
Widerhall fand. Sie würdigt seine Anteilnahme am deutschen Kulturerbe,
die er seit seinen Studien in Heidelberg in den Jahren 1890–1891 gezeigt hat.
Sie fühlt sich ihm dankbar verbunden.

Heidelberg, den 31. Mai des Jahres 1961, des 575. der Universität.

17 Klaus W. Jonas: *Der Kronprinz Wilhelm* (Frankfurt a. M., 1962). Englischer Text: *The Life of Crown Prince William*. (University of Pittsburgh Press, 1961).
18 Vgl. Klaus W. Jonas: Der Bildhauer Fritz Behn. In: Rolf Saltzwedel (Hrsg.): *Der Wagen. Ein Lübeckisches Jahrbuch* (Lübeck, 2000/2001), S. 190–214.

VILLA MAURESQUE,
ST. JEAN-CAP FERRAT,
A.M.

2nd February, 1965.

Dearest Doris and Klaus,

Thank you for your card and good wishes on my ninety-first birthday. It was extremely kind and sweet of you to remember me; I was very much touched and pleased.

The picture of the Polynesian virgin that you sent to Alan has had a very bad effect on him – he now wants to leave home.

Yours affectionately,

W. J. Maugham

Letzter Brief von W. Somerset Maugham, 2. Februar 1965

VILLA MAURESQUE
ST. JEAN CAP FERRAT
A-M

13th January, 1966.

Dear, dearest Doris and Klaus,

    Thank you for all your sympathy and understanding. It meant much to me, and I was deeply touched.

    Poor Mr. Maugham suffered so terribly during the last four years of his life that I was glad to see him go; but I miss him so dreadfully, and feel so lonely and lost and bewildered.

    I am going to London on the 18th for three weeks to settle a lot of business, then back here to clear up the house. After that the doctors say that unless I have three months complete rest I shall break down; so I plan to go to California for a while. I hope with all my heart that I shall see you during my stay in America.

    Once again a thousand thanks for your love and affection.

    Alan.

    Too broken to write any more.

Letzter Brief von Alan Searle, 13. Januar 1966

THE WRITER'S POINT OF VIEW

by

W. Somerset Maugham

for my old friend
Klaus Jonas

NATIONAL BOOK LEAGUE NINTH ANNUAL LECTURE

Widmung von Somerset Maugham

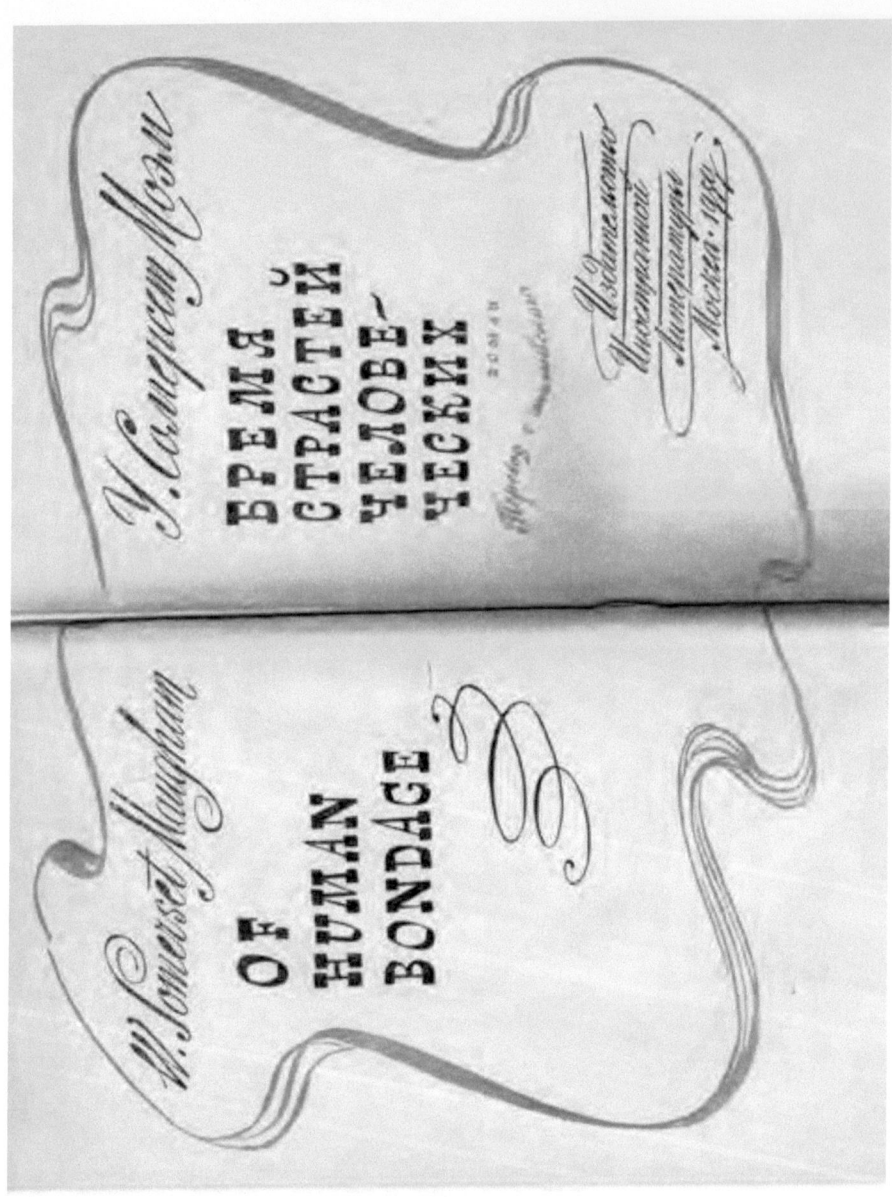

Titelblatt der russischen Übersetzung von *Of Human Bondage*

Widmung in russischer Übersetzung von *Of Human Bondage*

Widmung in *Horizon*, Bd. 1, Nr. 3 (Januar 1959)

Bibliography of Maugham's Own Literary Work
Somerset Maughams Werk

Romane – Novels

Liza of Lambeth (1897)
The Making of a Saint (1898)
The Hero (1901)
Mrs. Craddock (1902)
    Neuausgabe 1928
The Merry-Go-Round (1904)
The Bishop's Apron (1906)
The Explorer (1907)
The Magician (1908)
Of Human Bondage (1915)
    Neuausgabe 1946
The Moon and Sixpence (1919)
The Painted Veil (1925, 2006)
Cakes and Ale (1930)
The Narrow Corner (1932)
Theatre (1937, 2004)
Christmas Holiday (1939)
Up at the Villa (1941)
The Hour before the Dawn
    (New York, 1942)
The Razor's Edge (1944)
Then and Now (1946)
Catalina (1948)

Dramen – Plays

A Man of Honour (1903)
Mrs. Dot (1904)
Lady Frederick (1911)
Jack Straw (1911)
The Explorer (1912)
Penelope (1912)
The Tenth Man (1913)
Landed Gentry (1913)
Smith (1913)
The Land of Promise (1913)
The Unknown (1920)
The Circle (1921)
East of Suez (1922)
Caesar's Wife (1922)
Our Betters (1923)
Home and Beauty (1923)
The Unobtainable (1923)
Loaves and Fishes (1924)
The Letter (1927)
The Constant Wife (1927)
The Sacred Flame (1928)
The Breadwinner (1930)
For Services Rendered (1932)
Sheppey (1933)
The Noble Spaniard (1953)
The Plays of W. Somerset Maugham, 6 Bände (1931–1934)

Kurzgeschichten – Short Stories

Orientations (1899)
The Trembling of a Leaf (1921)
The Casuarina Tree (1926)
Ashenden (1928)
*Six Stories Written in the First
    Person Singular* (1931)

Ah King (1933)
Cosmopolitans (1936)
The Mixture as Before (1940)
Creatures of Circumstance (1947)

Gesammelte Kurzgeschichten – Collected Short Stories

Altogether (London, 1934), in
    USA unter dem Titel *East
    And West* (New York, 1934)

The Complete Short Stories
    (London, 1951, 3 Bände)

Verschiedenes (Reisen, Erinnerungen, Essays)
Miscellaneous (Travel Books, Memoirs, Essays)

The Land of the Blessed Virgin
    (1905)
On a Chinese Screen (1922)
The Gentleman in the Parlour
    (1930)
Don Fernando (1935)
The Summing Up (1938)
France at War (1940)
Books and You (1940)
Strictly Personal (1941)
A Writer's Notebook (1949)
The Vagrant Mood (1952)

Ten Novels and their Authors
    (1954)
The Writer's Point of View (1958)
Purely for my Pleasure (1962)
Looking Back (1962) (in der U.S.
    Zeitschrift *Show* und der Lon-
    doner Zeitung *The Sunday Ex-
    press*)
Loren R. Rothschild (Hrsg.): *The
    Letters of William Somerset
    Maugham to Lady Juliet Duff*
    (Pacific Palisades, 1982)

Verfilmungen – Film Adaptations

1925 – *The Circle* – mit Alec B. Francis nach der Komödie „Der Kreis" – Frank Borzage

1926 – Der Magier (*The Magician*) – Rex Ingram

1928 – Sadie Thompson – nach der Erzählung „Miss Thompson" – Raoul Walsh

1929 – *Charming Sinners* – nach „Finden Sie, daß Constanze sich richtig verhält?" – R. Milton

1930 – *Strictly Unconventional* – nach der Komödie „Der Kreis" – D. Burton

1932 – Regen (*Rain*) – Lewis Milestone

1934 – Der bunte Schleier (*The Painted Veil*) – Richard Boleslawski

1934 – *Of Human Bondage* – John Cromwell

1936 – Geheimagent (*The Secret Agent*) – Vorlage: Roman „Ashenden" – Alfred Hitchcock

1940 – Das Geheimnis von Malampur (*The Letter*) Vorlage: Kurzgeschichte „Der Brief" – William Wyler

1940 – Ein Ehemann zuviel (*Too many Husbands*) – Vorlage: Bühnenstück „Home and Beauty" – Wesley Ruggles

1942 – Der Besessene von Tahiti (*The Moon and Sixpence*) – Vorlage: Roman „Silbermond und Kupfermünze" – Albert Lewin

1944 – Weihnachtsurlaub (*Christmas Holiday*) – Robert Siodmak

1946 – *Of Human Bondage* – Edmund Goulding

1946 – Auf Messers Schneide (*The Razor's Edge*) – nach dem gleichnamigen Bühnenstück – Edward Goulding

1947 – Ehebruch (*The Unfaithful*) – Remake von „Das Geheimnis von Malampur" – Vincent Sherman

1948 – Quartett (*Quartet*) – Vorlage: die Novellen „The facts of life", „The Alien Corn", „The Kite", „The Colonel's Lady" – Ken Annakin, Ralph Smart, Harold French, Arthur Crabtree

1950 – So ist das Leben (*Trio*) – Vorlage: drei Novellen – Ken Annakin, Harold French

1951 – Dakapo (*Encore*) – Vorlage: Erzählungen „The Ant and the Grasshopper", „Winter Cruise", „Gigolo and Gigolette" – Pat Jackson, Harold French, Anthony Pelissier

1953 – Fegefeuer (*Miss Sadie Thompson*) – Vorlage: Erzählung „Miss Thompson" – Curtis Bernhardt

1954 – Ins Paradies verdammt (*The Beachcomber*) – Muriel Box

1954 – Liebe im Quartett (*Three for the Show*) – Remake von „Too many Husbands" – Henry C. Potter

1954/55 – Mord ohne Mörder (*Three Cases of Murder*) – Vorlage: „Lord Mountdrago" und zwei weitere Novellen – Wendy Toye, David Eady und George More O'Ferrall

1957 – Hongkong war ihr Schicksal (*The Seventh Sin*) – Vorlage: Roman „Der bunte Schleier" – Ronald Neame

1961 – Julia, Du bist zauberhaft (*Adorable Julie*) – Alfred Weidenmann

1962 – Finden Sie, daß Constanze sich richtig verhält? – Tom Pevsner

1962 – Heute kündigt mir mein Mann (Vorlage: Bühnenstück „The Breadwinner") – Rudolf Nussgruber, Peter Goldbaum

1964 – Der Menschen Hörigkeit (*Of Human Bondage*) – Ken Hughes, Bryan Forbes, Henry Hathaway

1981 – Der verhängnisvolle Brief (*The Letter*) – Remake von „Das Geheimnis von Malampur" – John Erman

1984 – Auf Messers Schneide (*The Razor's Edge*) – nach dem gleichnamigen Bühnenstück – John Byrum

2000 – Die Villa (*Up at the Villa*) – Philip Haas

2004 – Being Julia – Vorlage: Roman „*Theater*" – István Szabó

2006 – *The Painted Veil* – Vorlage: Roman „Der bunte Schleier" – John Curran – mit Naomi Watts als Kitty und Edward Norton als Walter

In den mehr als dreißig zwischen 1925 und 2006 erschienenen Filmen traten einige der bekanntesten Schauspieler auf wie:

Billie Burke (1917)	Humphry Bogart (1936)
Ethel Barrymore (1919)	Charles Laughton (1938)
Pola Negri (1924)	Dirk Bogarde (1948)
Paul Wegener (1926)	Jean Simmons (1950)
Gloria Swanson (1928)	Rita Hayworth (1953)
Joan Crawford (1932)	José Ferrer (1953)
John Huston (1932)	Orson Welles (1954)
Douglas Fairbanks (1933)	Lilli Palmer (1962)
Bette Davis (1934)	Charles Boyer (1962)
Greta Garbo (1934)	Kim Novak (1964)
Gene Kelly (1934)	

Bibliography of Secondary Literature
Literatur über Somerset Maugham

Aldington, Richard:

W. Somerset Maugham. Novelist, Essayist, Dramatist. With a Preface by W. Somerset Maugham (New York, 1939).

W. Somerset Maugham: An Appreciatation (New York, 1939). Aus: *Saturday Review* (London), Jg. 20 (19. August 1939), S. 3–4, 12.

Somerset Maugham: An Appreciation of the Author. In: *Wisdom*, Vol. 2, No. 4 (April 1957), S. 16–19.

Somerset Maugham. In: Alister Kershaw (Hrsg.): *Selected Critical Writings 1928–1960* (Carbondale, Illinois, 1970).

Aldridge, John W.:

Mr. Maugham's ten sheared Candidates. In: *Saturday Review of Literature*, Bd. 31 (2. Oktober 1948), S. 23–24 [*Great Novelists and their Novels*].

Allen, Walter:

Summing up Somerset Maugham at 90. In: *New York Times Book Review*, 19. Januar 1964, S. 1, 24.

Allsop, Kenneth:

K.A. remembers a Meeting with S.M., Enjoying the Truce of Old Age. In: *Books and Bookmen*, Bd. 10 (Mai 1966), S. 18, 55 [Interview].

Alpert, Hollis:

Dean of the Smoothies. In: *Saturday Review* (New York), Bd. 36 (25. April 1953), S. 21 [*The Vagrant Mood*].

Altman, Wilfred:

Somerset Maugham: An Appreciation. In: *Contemporary Review*, Bd. 208 (Februar 1966), S. 99–104.

Amis, Kingsly:

> Mr. Maugham's Notions. In: *Spectator*, Bd. 207 (7. Juli 1961), S. 23–24 [*Cakes and Ale – Of Human Bondage*].

Anderson, Maxwell:

> In Vishnu-Land What Avatar? *The Moon and Sixpence*. In: K.W. Jonas, *The Maugham Enigma* (1954), S. 129–132.

Angoff, Charles:

> The Library: W. Somerset Maugham. In: *The American Mercury*, Bd. 70 (Januar 1950), S. 111–117. [*A Writer's Notebook*].

Anon.:

> Maugham Mauled. In: *Time*, Jg. 17 (13. April 1931), S. 79–80. Betrifft *Gin and Bitters* von A. Riposte [Pseud. von Elinor Mordaunt].

> *Gin and Bitters* held up: English Edition is called off after Friends of Maugham protest. In: *New York Times*, 7. Mai 1931, S. 26 [Betrifft Elinor Mordaunts Satire *Gin and Bitters* – vgl. *New York Times*, 14. Mai 1931].

> Mr. Maugham's Novels. In: *Times Literary Supplement*, 19. Juli 1934, S. 506 [*Liza of Lambeth – The Painted Veil – Ashenden – Cakes and Ale*].

> Books: Old Man with a Razor. In: *Time*, Bd. 43 (24. April 1944), S. 99–100, 102 [*The Razor's Edge*].

> Table Talk at 79. In: *Time*, Bd. 61 (6. April 1953), S. 117–118, 120.

> The New Somerset Maugham. In: *Holiday*, Februar 1954, S. 16, 18.

> Somerset Maugham: Bücher als Telegramme. In: *Der Spiegel*, Jg. 12, Nr. 15 (11. April 1956), S. 34–42.

> Somerset Maugham Makes a very odd Request. In: *Daily Mail*, 12. November 1957, S. 12.

> [BN.]: Erzählen aus Leidenschaft und Beruf. In: *Bremer Nachrichten*, Nr. 294 (17. Dezember 1965), S. 14.

> Somerset Maugham gestorben. In: *Neue Zürcher Zeitung*, 17. Dezember 1965.

> Mort de Somerset Maugham. In: *Le Figaro*, 17. Dezember 1965, S. 1, 21 [Nachruf].

Mr. Somerset Maugham: The most assured Writer of his Time. In: *Times* (17. Dezember 1965), S. 17 [Nachruf].

Somerset Maugham is dead at 91. In: *New York Times*, 17. Dezember 1965, S. 1, 50 [Nachruf].

Archer, Stanley:

W. Somerset Maugham. A Study of the Short Fiction (New York, 1993).

Auden, Wystan H.:

Notebooks of Somerset Maugham. In: *New York Times Book Review*, 23. Oktober 1949, S. 1, 22 [*A Writer's Notebook*].

Barber, Noël:

The New Somerset Maugham. In: *Holiday*, Jg. 15, Nr. 2 (Februar 1954), S. 15–16, 18–20.

Barnes, Ronald Edgar:

The Dramatic Comedy of William Somerset Maugham (Den Haag, Paris, 1968).

Bason, Frederick T.:

A Bibliography of the Writings of William Somerset Maugham (London, 1931).

Mr. Somerset Maugham. In: *Saturday Book, Fifth Year* (Oktober 1945), S. 279–284.

W. Somerset Maugham. In Noël Coward (Hrsg.): *The last Bassoon* (London, 1960), S. 8, 34–35, 36, 88, 102, 132.

Postscript to Maugham. In: *The Saturday Book*, (London, 1966), S. 185–188 [Nachruf].

Basso, Hamilton:

W. Somerset Maugham: A Profile. In: *The New Yorker*, Bd. 30 (30. Dezember 1944, 6. Januar 1945), S. 24–38.

Beach, Joseph Warren:

Maugham considers Mystics. In: *New York Times Book Review*, 23. April 1944, S. 3 [*The Razor's Edge*].

Beaton, Cecil:

The Glass of Fashion (Garden City, New York, 1954).

The Villa Mauresque and Somerset Maugham, In: *The Strenuous Years: Diaries, 1948–1955* (London, 1973).

Beavan, John:

Maugham: A „Free Man" at 85. In: *New York Times*, 25. Januar 1959, S. 14, 34–35, 37 [Interview].

Beerbohm, Max:

A Parenthesis: W. Somerset Maugham. In: *Saturday Review* (London), Bd. 106 (9. Januar 1909), S. 39–40.

Behrman, S.N.:

Books: Notes of a Popular Pessimist. In: *The New Yorker*, Bd. 25 (29. Oktober 1949), S. 88, 91–94 [*A Writer's Notebook*].

Maugham, Playwright. In: *New York Times*, 2. Januar 1966, Sektion II, S. 1, 3 [*Our Betters – The Circle*].

W. Somerset Maugham. In: *People in a Diary: A Memoir* (Boston, 1972), S. 276–312.

Belloc, Elizabeth:

The Stories of Somerset Maugham. In: *Month*, Bd. 218 (Juli – August 1964), S. 67–72.

Bender, J. Terry:

Stanford University Library: A Comprehensive Exhibition of the Writings of W. Somerset Maugham 25. Mai – 1. August 1958 [Ausstellungskatalog], Mit einem Vorwort von W. Somerset Maugham.

Benét, Stephen Vincent:

A Self-Taught Trade. In: *Saturday Review of Literature*, Bd. 17 (16. April 1938), S. 3–4 [*The Summing Up – Of Human Bondage*].

Benét, William Rose:

English Maupassant. In: *Saturday Review of Literature*, Bd. 22 (27. Juli 1940), S. 10 [*The Mixture as Before*].

Maughamana, 1892–1949. In: *Saturday Review of Literature*, Bd. 32 (22. Oktober 1949), S. 16–17 [*A Writer's Notebook*].

Berthoud, Roger:

Graham Sutherland: A Biography (London, 1982), S. 141–142.

Boothby, Lord [Robert John Graham]:

The Maugham „Legend". In: *My Yesterday, Your Tomorrow* (London, 1962), S. 224–228.

Brady, Thomas F.:

The Eighty Years of Mr. Maugham. In: *New York Times*, 24. Januar 1954, S. 12, 52, 53 [Interview].

Brandner, Laurence:

Somerset Maugham: A Guide (Edinburgh, New York, 1963).

Breit, Harvey:

Talk with Two Writers. In: *New York Times Book Review*, 19. November 1950, S. 39 [Maugham und Evelyn Waugh].

Brenner, Anita:

A Gentleman and his Personality. In: *The Nation* (New York), Bd. 141 (21. August 1935), S. 221 [*Don Fernando*].

Britten, Florence Haxton:

Maugham's Tragic Tales. In: *New York Herald Tribune Books*, 12. November 1933, S. 4 [*Ah King*].

Cosmopolitans. In: *New York Herald Tribune Books*, 23. Februar 1936, S. 10 [*Cosmopolitans*].

Brooks, Cleanth, und Robert B. Heilmann:

The Circle by Somerset Maugham. In: *Understanding Drama: Twelve Plays*, New York, 1963, S. 12–15.

Brophy, John:

Somerset Maugham (London, New York, 1952).

Brown, Allen B.:

W. Somerset Maugham as a Novelist. Dissertation, State University of Iowa, 1953.

Substance and Shadow: The Original of the Characters in *Cakes and Ale.* In: *Papers of the Michigan Academy of Science, Art and Letters*, Bd. 45 (1960), S. 439–446 [*Cakes and Ale*].

Brown, Ivor:

William, half a Conqueror. In: *Drama*, Bd. 81 (Sommer 1966), S. 25–26.

Brown, John Mason:

English Laughter – Past and Present. In: *Saturday Review of Literature*, Bd. 29 (23. November 1946), S. 24–26, auch in *Dramatis Personae: A Retrospective Show* (New York, 1963), S. 183–190.

Bunting, John J., Jr.:

W. Somerset Maugham and the Christian Preacher. In: *Religion in Life*, Bd. 21 (Sommer 1952), S. 401–410.

Burgess, Anthony:

Introduction to Maugham's Malaysian Stories (Hong Kong, 1969), VI–XVII.

W. Somerset Maugham: 1874–1965. In: *Listener*, Bd. 74 (23. Dezember 1965), S. 1033 [Nachruf].

Burt, Forrest D.:

A New Methodology for Psychological Criticism of Literature: A Case Study for William Somerset Maugham. Dissertation, Texas Technological College, 1967.

Calder, Robert:

W. Somerset Maugham and the Quest for Freedom (Garden City, New York, 1973).

Willie. The Life of W. Somerset Maugham (New York, 1989).

Canby, Henry Seidel:

The Soul of Spain. In: *Saturday Review of Literature*, Bd. 12 (27. Juli 1935), S. 7 [*Don Fernando*].

Cantwell, Robert:

With a superior Sense of Reality. In: *New York Times Book Review*, 24. April 1955, S. 4.

Vgl. *The Art of Fiction: An Introduction to Ten Novels and their Authors.* In: *Harper's Magazine*, Bd. 210, Nr. 1 (Mai 1955), S. 84, 86.

de Carbuccia, Horace:

Adieu à mon ami anglais. In: *Gringoire*, 7. November 1941, S. 1–2 [als Pamphlet erschienen: Paris, 1942].

Cecil, Hugh und Mirabel:

Clever Hearts: Desmond and Molly MacCarthy (London, 1991).

Cerf, Benet A.:

The Razor's Edge. In: *Saturday Review of Literature*, 27. Mai 1944.

Chambrun, Jacques:

Mr. Maugham's Magic Cup. In: *Reader's Digest*, Dezember 1954, S. 10.

Chappelow, Alan:

Interview with Maugham. In: *Daily Mail* (London), 21. Januar 1954.

Chubb, Thomas C.:

Maugham's Machiavelli. In: *New York Times Book Review*, 26. Mai 1946, S. 4 [*Then and Now*].

Cierpal, Leo Joseph:

Degeneration and the Religion of Beauty: A Traditional Pattern in Coleridge's „*The Rime of the Ancient Mariner*", Pater's „*The Renaissance*", Maugham's „*Of Human Bondage*", and Joyce's „*Ulysses*". Dissertation, Wayne State University, 1962.

Clark, Kenneth:

The Other Half: A Self-Portrait (Toronto, 1977), S. 116.

Clinton, Farley:

Men and Letters: Maugham's Bondage. In: *National Review* (New York), Bd. 18 (22. Februar 1966), S. 174–176 [Nachruf].

Cody, Richard:

Secret Service Fiction. In: *Graduate Student of English*, Bd. 3 (Sommer 1960), S. 6–12 [*Ashenden*].

Colburn, William E.:

Dr. Maugham's Prescription for Success. In: *Emory University Quarterly*, Bd. 19 (Frühjahr 1963), S. 14–21 [*Liza of Lambeth*].

Collins, W.P.:

W. Somerset Maugham. Playwright and Novelist. *Bookman* (London), Jg. 57 (Oktober 1919), S. 12–15.

Colum, Mary M.:

The Book Forum. In: *Forum*, Bd. 97 (Mai 1937), S. iv [*Theatre*].

Life and Literature. In: *Forum*, Bd. 111 (Dezember 1939), S. 260–261 [*Christmas Holiday*].

Comden, Betty:

Maugham and the Movies. In: *New York Times Book Review* (29. März 1949), S. 4, 18 [*Quartet*].

Connolly, Cyril:

The Art of being Good. In: *New Statesman and Nation*, N.S. Bd. 28 (26. August 1944), S. 140, auch in *The Condemned Playground-Essays 1927–1944* (New York, 1945), S. 250–254 [*Cakes and Ale – The Razor's Edge*].

Maugham: Compassionate Cynic. In: *The Sunday Times*. 19. Dezember 1965, S. 35 [Nachruf].

Connon, Bryan:

Somerset Maugham and the Maugham Dynasty (London, 1989, 1997).

Cordell, Richard A.:

W. Somerset Maugham (New York, 1937).

Five-Day Adventure. In: *Saturday Review of Literature*, Bd. 20 (21. Oktober 1939), S. 10 [*Christmas Holiday*].

Our Betters. In: K.W. Jonas, *The Maugham Enigma* (1954), S. 107–110.

The Constant Wife. In: K.W. Jonas, *The Maugham Enigma* (1954), S. 111–113.

The Narrow Corner. In: K.W. Jonas, *The Maugham Enigma* (1954), S. 149–152.

Teller of Tales: Somerset Maugham's Short Stories. In: K.W. Jonas, *The Maugham Enigma* (1954), S. 167–170.

The Trembling of a Leaf. In: K.W. Jonas, *The Maugham Enigma* (1954), S. 171–176.

The Gentleman in the Parlour. In: K.W. Jonas, *The Maugham Enigma* (1954), S. 197–199.

Somerset Maugham: Lucidity versus Cunning. In: *English Fiction in Transition*, Bd. 1, Nr. 3 (Herbst 1958), S. 30–32.

The Theatre of Somerset Maugham. In: *Modern Drama,* Bd. 1 (Februar 1959), S. 211–217 [*The Circle – Our Betters – The Constant Wife*].

Somerset Maugham: A Biographical and Critical Study (London, Bloomington, 1961).

Somerset Maugham. A Writer for all Seasons (Bloomington, Indiana, 1969).

Cosman, Max:

Mr. Maugham as Footnote. In: *Pacific Spectator*, Bd. 10 (Winter 1956), S. 64–69.

Coulter, Stephen:

Maugham at Ninety. In: *Sunday Times* (London), 19. Januar 1964, S. 30.

Coward, Noël:

In: Graham Pays and Sheridan Morley (Hrsg.): *Diaries* (Boston, 1982).

Cowley, Malcolm:

Angry Author's Complaint. In: *The New Republic*, Bd. 80 (22. August 1934), S. 51–52, auch in K.W. Jonas, *The Maugham Enigma* (1954), S. 180–184 [*East and West*].

The Maugham Enigma. In: *The New Republic*, Bd. 94 (30. März 1938), S. 227–228. Auch in: K.W. Jonas, *The Maugham Enigma* (1954), S. 200–204 [*Of Human Bondage*].

Personal Histories. In: *The New Republic*, Bd. 105 (15. September 1941), S. 345–346 [*Strictly Personal*].

The Devil a Monk was he. In: *The New Republic*, Bd. 110 (1. Mai 1944), S. 609 [*The Razor's Edge*].

Craven, H.T.:

Tahiti from Melville to Maugham. In: *Bookman* (New York), Bd. 50 (November 1919), S. 262–267 [*The Moon and Sixpence*].

Cuff, Sergeant:

Criminal Record. In: *Saturday Review* (New York), Bd. 49 (25. Juni 1966), S. 31 [*Ashenden*].

Cukor, George:

Remembering Maugham (Los Angeles, 1966).

Curtis, Anthony:

The Pattern of Maugham (London, 1974).

Somerset Maugham (New York, 1977).

Curtis, Anthony und John Whitehead (Hrsg.):

W. Somerset Maugham: The Critical Heritage (London, 1987).

Cyriax, Rolf:

Der Dramatiker William Somerset Maugham (Freiburg i. Br., 1968).

Dangerfield, George:

Fiction. In: *Bookman* (New York), Bd. 73 (Mai 1931), S. 320–321, Betrifft *Gin and Bitters* von A. Riposte [Pseud. von Elinor Mordaunt].

Diary of a New Dimension. In: *Saturday Review of Literature*, Jg. 24 (13. September 1941), S. 13 [*Strictly Personal*].

Daruwalla, Bejan:

Somerset Maugham as a Teller of Tales. In: *Modern Review* (Calcutta), Bd. 109 (Januar 1961), S. 55–58.

Davies, Horton:

W. Somerset Maugham. In: *A Mirror of the Ministry in Modern Novels* (New York, 1959), S. 113–122 [„Rain" – *Of Human Bondage*].

Davies, H.M.P.:

The King's School, Canterbury: The Hugh Walpole Collection: The Somerset Maugham Library. In: *Études Anglaises*, Bd. 16 (Januar – März 1963), S. 59–62.

Dennis, Nigel:

Up at the Villa. In: *New Republic*, Bd. 104 (19. Mai 1941), S. 704 [*Up at the Villa*].

DeVoto, Bernard:

Master of Two Dimensions. In: *Saturday Review of Literature*, Bd. 15 (6. März 1937), S. 3 [*Theatre*].

Dickie, Francis:

From Forest Fire to France: Somerset Maugham and his Moorish Mansion. In: *American Book Collector*, Bd. 10, Nr. 7 (März 1959), S. 7, 9, 11, 13 [Interview].

Dietrich, Margret:

Das moderne Drama: Strömungen, Gestalten, Motive (Stuttgart, 1963), S. 71, 77–78, 79, 677.

Dobrinsky, Joseph:

Aspects biographiques de l'œuvre de Somerset Maugham: l'enfance. In: *Études Anglaises*, Bd. 8 (Oktober/Dezember 1955), S. 299–312.

Les Débuts de Somerset Maugham au Théâtre. In: *Études Anglaises*, Bd. 10 (Oktober bis Dezember 1957), S. 310–321, [Résumé unter dem gleichen Titel, Dissertation, Universität Montpellier, 1955].

La jeunesse de Somerset Maugham (1874–1903). Paris, 1976. (Études Anglaises, 62)

Dolch, Martin:
Somerset Maugham. In: John V. Hagopian und Martin Dolch (Hrsg.): *Insight II: Analyses of Modern British Literature* (Frankfurt, 1964), S. 251–259 [*The Outstation*].

Doner, Dean:

Spinoza's Ethics and Maugham. In: *University of Kansas City Review*, Bd. 21 (Juni 1955), S. 261–269 [*Of Human Bondage*].

Dottin, Paul:

Le Réalisme de Somerset Maugham. In: *La Revue de France*, Bd. 6, Nr. 3 (1. Juni 1926), S. 574–581.

Englische Übersetzung in: K.W. Jonas, *The Maugham Enigma* (1954), S. 133–145. The Realism of Somerset Maugham: *The Painted Veil*.

W. Somerset Maugham et ses romans (Paris, 1928).

Les Lettres Étrangères: Somerset Maugham, Romancier satirique. In: *La Revue de France*, Jg. 12, Nr. 2 (1. April 1932), S. 565–571 [*Cakes and Ale*].

Le Théatre de Somerset Maugham (Paris, 1937).

Doubleday, Ellen:

In: W. Somerset Maugham: An Appreciation with Biographical Sketches and a Bibliography (Garden City, New York, 1965).

Dreiser, Theodore:

As a Realist sees it. In: *The New Republic*, Bd. 5 (25. Dezember 1915), S. 202–204 [*Of Human Bondage*]. Auch in: K.W. Jonas, *The Maugham Enigma* (1954), S. 114–120.

Eaton, Walter Prichard:

Playwright who stumbled into Fame. In: *Harper's Weekly*, Jg. 52, Nr. 32 (10. Oktober 1908). Auch in: K.W. Jonas, *The Maugham Enigma* (1954), S. 101–103.

Maugham in the Process of Becoming. In: *New York Herald Tribune*, 23. Oktober 1949, S. 5 [*A Writer's Notebook*].

Edel, Leon:

Of Willie's Bondage. In: *Saturday Review*, 15. März 1980, S. 36.

Editorial:

Somerset Maugham at 80. In: *New York Times*, 25. Januar 1954, S. 18.

Edman, Irwin:

The Philosopher as Man of Letters. In: *Proceedings of the American Academy of Arts and Letters,* Second Series, Nr. 1 (New York, 1951), S. 69–72. Auch in: K.W. Jonas, *The Maugham Enigma* (1954), S. 50–53.

Epstein, Joseph:

Epstein: *An Autobiography* (London, 1955), S. 235.

Is it all right to read Somerset Maugham? In: *Partial Payments* (New York, 1989), S. 185–209.

Ervine, St. John:

The Plays of W. Somerset Maugham. In: *Life and Letters*, Bd. 11 (März 1935), S. 640–655. Unter dem Titel: *Maugham the Playwright*, in K.W. Jonas, *The World of Somerset Maugham* (1959), S. 142–162.

Fadiman, Clifton:

Books: Mr. Maugham's Mixture. In: *New Yorker*, Bd. 16 (13. Juli 1940), S. 60–61 [*The Mixture as Before*].

Farrar, John:

W. Somerset Maugham: Novelist and so forth. In: *Charles Hanson Towne* (New York, 1925), S. 5–7.

Farrelly, John:

Fiction Parade. In: *New Republic*, Bd. 117 (11. August 1947), S. 30–32 [*Creatures of Circumstance*].

Farson, Daniel:

Christmas at the Villa Mauresque. In: *Sacred Memories* (London, 1988), S. 11–30.

Feld, Rose:

Somerset Maugham's War Novel. In: *New York Herald Tribune Books*, 21. Juni 1942, S. 4 [*The Hour before the Dawn*].

A Quest for the Absolute. In: *New York Herald Tribune Weekly Book Review*, 23. April 1944, S. 19 [*The Razor's Edge*].

Field, Louise M.:

Maugham's Chinese Sketches. In: *New York Times Book Review*, 4. Februar 1923, S. 11. Auch in: K.W. Jonas, *The Maugham Enigma* (1954), S. 191–193 [*On a Chinese Screen*].

Fielden, John Seward:

William Somerset Maugham, the Dramatist. Dissertation, Boston University, 1954.

Mrs. Beamish and *The Circle*. In: *Boston University Studies in English*, Bd. 2 (Sommer 1956), S. 113–123 [Über ein unveröffentlichtes Manuskript im Vergleich zum Drama *The Circle*].

Somerset Maugham on the Purpose of Drama. In: *Educational Theatre Journal*, Bd. 10 (Oktober 1958), S. 218–222.

The Ibsenite Maugham. In: *Modern Drama*, Bd. 4 (September 1961), S. 138–151.

Fisher, Richard:

Syrie Maugham (London, 1978).

Fleming, Ann:

W. Somerset Maugham. In: Mark Amory (Hrsg.): *Letters* (London, 1985).

Fogg, Derek:

Somerset Maugham in Heidelberg. In: *Ruperto-Carola*, IX, Bd. 21 (Juni 1957), S. 178. – Vgl. *Ruperto-Carola*, XIII, Bd. 30 (Dezember 1961), S. 40, 42.

Ford, George H.:

W. Somerset Maugham. In: *Dickens and his Readers: Aspects of Novel Criticism since 1836* (Princeton, 1955), S. 160, 191, 195, 224, 225.

Fricker, Robert:

Das moderne englische Drama (Göttingen, 1964), S. 11, 15, 29–30, 32, 52, 68, 78 [*Our Betters – The Circle – The Breadwinner – The Constant Wife*].

Gerber, Helmut E.:

W. Somerset Maugham. In: *The English Short Story in Transition*: 1880–1920 (New York, 1967), S. 425–426, 510–511.

Gibney, Robert:

Then and Now: Somerset Maugham. In: *Vogue*, Bd. 108 (Juli 1946), S. 94, 132–134 [*Then and Now*].

Gilroy, Harry:

How to write – by Maugham. In: *New York Times Magazine*, 23. Januar 1949, S. 10, 41–42. Auch in: K.W. Jonas, *The Maugham Enigma* (1954), S. 41–49 [Interview].

Posthumous Publications barred by Maugham's Executor [Alexander S. Frere] In: *New York Times*, 16. Dezember 1965, S. 50.

Goodrich, Marcus Aurelius:

After Ten Years *Of Human Bondage*. In: *New York Times Book Review*, 25. Januar 1925, S. 2. Auch in: *Charles Hanson Towne* (New York, 1925), S. 37–44.

Gordon, Caroline:

Notes on Chekhov and Maugham. In: *Sewanee Review*, Bd. 57 (Sommer 1949), S. 401–410.

How to read a Novel (New York, 1957), S. 117–118 [*Christmas Holiday*].

Gordon, John D.:

New in the Berg Collection, 1957–1958. In: *Bulletin of the New York Public Library*, Bd. 63 (März 1959), S. 134–147 [*The Razor's Edge*].

Gordon, Ruth:

Myself among Others (New York, 1971).

Goren, Charles:

Maugham never forgot the Day I trumped his Ace. In: *Sports Illustrated*, Bd. 24 (17. Januar 1966), S. 50–51.

Grace, William J.:

Seeing the War. In: *Commonweal*, Bd. 34 (10. Oktober 1941), S. 594–595 [*Strictly Personal*].

Gray, James:

Obituary of the Human Race. In: *On Second Thought* (Minneapolis, London, 1946), S. 165–183 [*Of Human Bondage – Rain*].

Green, Julien:

Über einen Besuch bei Somerset Maugham im April 1952. In: *Journal*, 1950–1954 (Paris, 1955), S. 154 [Französisch].

Greene, Graham:

Books of the Day: Maugham's Short Stories. In: *Spectator* (London), Bd. 153 (31. August 1934), S. 297.

Books of the Day: Spanish Gold, In: *Spectator* (London), Bd. 154 (21. Juni 1935), S. 1076. Unter dem Titel „Some Notes on Somerset Maugham" in *Collected Essays* (New York, 1969), S. 197–199 [*Don Fernando*]. Auch in: K.W. Jonas, *The Maugham Enigma* (1954), S. 194–196 [*Don Fernando*].

Books of the Day: Short Stories. In: *Spectator* (London), Bd. 156 (17. April 1936), S. 718–720 [*Cosmopolitans*].

Books of the Day: Maugham's Pattern. In: *Spectator* (London), Bd. 160 (14. Januar 1938), S. 59, Unter dem Titel „Some Notes on Somerset

Maugham" in *Collected Essays* (New York, 1969), S. 202–205 [*The Summing Up*].

Underworld. In: *London Mercury*, Bd. 39 (März 1939), S. 550–551 [*Christmas Holiday – Cakes and Ale*].

Some Notes on Somerset Maugham. In: *Collected Essays* (New York, 1979), S. 197–205.

Grötz, Alfred:

W. Somerset Maughams Erzählung „The Outstation". In: *Die Neueren Sprachen*, N.S., Bd. 6 (1957), S. 367–371 [Vergleich mit Galsworthy's *The Man who kept his Form*].

Guéry, Suzanne:

La Philosophie de Somerset Maugham (Paris, 1933).

Gumpert, Martin:

Ten who know the Secret of Age. In: *New York Times Magazine* (27. Dezember 1953), S. 10.

Haas, Willy:

Ein Kenner der Leidenschaften. Zum Tode von Somerset Maugham. In: *Die Welt*, Nr. 293 (17. Dezember 1965), S. 9.

Hammersley, Violet:

A Childhood in Paris. In: *John Lehmann* (Hrsg.) *Orpheus II* (London, 1949), S. 186.

Hassall, Christopher:

A Biography of Edward Marsh (New York, 1959).

Hastings, Selina:

The Secret Lives of Somerset Maugham. London: John Murray, 2009. New York: Random House, 2010.

Hauser, Marianne:

A Maugham Story. In: *New York Times Book Review*, 6. April 1941, S. 7 [*Up at the Villa*].

Henderson, Peter:

W. Somerset Maugham, 1889–1989, In: *The Cantuarian* (August 1989).

Henry, William H. Jr.:

A French Bibliography of W. Somerset Maugham (Charlottesville, Virginia, 1967).

Heywood, C.:

Somerset Maugham's Debt to *Madame Bovary* and Miss Braddon's *The Doctor's Wife*. In: *Études Anglaises*, Bd. 19 (Januar bis März 1966), S. 64–69.

Two printed Texts of Somerset Maugham's *Mrs. Craddock*. In: *English Language Notes*, Bd. 5 (September 1967), S. 39–46.

Hillyer, Dorothy:

Mr. Maugham on Men, Women. In: *New York Herald Tribune Books*, 6. April 1941, S. 2 [*Up at the Villa*].

Hines, Jack:

Mr. Maugham on Deck and in the Smoking Room. In: *New York Times Book Review*, 17. Juni 1923, S. 7 [Interview].

Holden, Philip:

Orienting Masculinity, Orienting Nation. W. Somerset Maugham's exotic Fiction (Westport, Conn., 1996).

Holliday, Terence:

Man of Letters. In: *Saturday Review of Literature*, Bd. 17 (26. März 1938), S. 5 [*The Summing Up*].

Horgan, Paul:

Luncheon with Somerset Maugham. In: *The American Scholar*, Nr. 62 (1993), S. 100.

Hughes, Richard:

Tokyo en Fête for Maugham. In: *Sunday Times*, 15. November 1959.

Hutchinson, Percy:

Maugham's Short Short-Stories. In: *New York Times Book Review*, 23. Februar 1936, S. 4 [*Cosmopolitans*].

Maugham's Portrait of a Woman. In: *New York Times Book Review*, 14. März 1937, S. 4 [*Theatre*].

Isherwood, Christopher:

Christopher and his Kind: 1929–1939. (New York, 1976), S. 325–327.

W. Somerset Maugham. In: Katherine Bucknell (Hrsg.): *Diaries: Volume One, 1939–1960* (New York, 1997).

Jack, Peter M.:

Somerset Maugham Sums up. In: *New York Times Book Review*, 27. März 1938, S. 2, 19 [*The Summing Up*].

Somerset Maugham's New Novel is One of his Best. In: *New York Times Book Review*, 22. Oktober 1939, S. 6 [*Christmas Holiday*].

The New Novels of Fiction. In: *New York Times Book Review*, 21. Juni 1942, S. 6 [*The Hour before the Dawn*].

James, Robert Rhodes:

Henry Wellcome (London, 1994).

Jensen, Sven Arnold:

William Somerset Maugham: Some Aspects of the Man and his Work (Oslo University Press, 1957).

Johnson, Edgar:

Growing Pains. In: *The New Republic*, Bd. 101 (8. November 1939), S. 21–22 [*Christmas Holiday*].

Jonas, Klaus W.:

A Bibliography of the Writings of W. Somerset Maugham (South Hadley, Mass., 1950).

W. Somerset Maugham und der Ferne Osten. Dissertation, Universität Münster, 1953.

W. Somerset Maugham. In: *Archiv für das Studium der Neueren Sprachen*, Bd. 189 (1953), S. 326–330. Auch in: *Die Neueren Sprachen*, N.S. Bd. 3 (1954), S. 543–548.

The Maugham Enigma (London, New York, 1954).

The Gentleman from Cap Ferrat (New Haven, Conn., 1956). Auch in: K.W. Jonas: *The World of Somerset Maugham* (New York, 1959), S. 21–36.

Biographical Portrait of a Writer: Somerset Maugham. In: *Wisdom*, Vol. 2, No. 4 (April 1957), S. 12–15.

Somerset Maugham at 84. In: *Gentlemen's Quarterly*, Bd. 28, Nr. 1 (1958), S. 64–65, 108, 111–114.

W. Somerset Maugham Collections in America. In: *Jahrbuch für Amerikastudien*, Bd. 3 (1958), S. 205–213.

A Note on Maugham Collections. In: *The World of Somerset Maugham* (New York, 1959), S. 180–194.

The Center of Maugham Studies. In:

Stechert-Hafner Book News, Bd. 13 (5. Januar 1959), S. 53–55.

The World of Somerset Maugham (London, New York 1959. Reprint Edition: Westport, Conn., 1972). Japanische Übersetzung durch Mutsuo Tanaka (Tokio, 1959).

W. Somerset Maugham: An Appreciation. In: *Books Abroad*, Bd. 33 (Winter 1959), S. 20–23.

Begegnungen in Amerika: Thomas Mann und W. Somerset Maugham. In: *Die Tat* (Zürich), Jg. 38, Nr. 168 (21. Juli 1973), S. 21. Auch in: *Rheinischer Merkur* (Koblenz), Jg. 29, Nr. 31 (2. August 1974), Aus dem Leben des Geistes, S. 16.

Kanin, Garson:

Remembering Mr. Maugham. In: *Vogue*, Bd. 148 (15. August 1966), S. 86–87, 133–134, 136 [Vorabdruck aus Kanins Band mit dem gleichen Titel: *Remembering Mr. Maugham*. Vorwort von Noël Coward (New York, 1966)].

Kelly, Sir Gerald:

Old Friends. In: *Sunday Times*, 24. Januar 1954, S. 6.

Kendall, Lyle H. Jr.:

The First Edition of *The Moon and Sixpence*. In: *Papers of the Bibliographical Society of America*, Bd. 55 (Third Quarter 1961), S. 242–243.

King, Francis:

Yesterday came Suddenly (London, 1993).

Klein, R.:

A Producer to a Playwright. A Letter to Somerset Maugham. *London Mercury*, Bd. 38 (Mai 1938), S. 16–26 [*The Summing Up*].

Knecht, Jean:

Somerset Maugham, un maître de l'humour élégant et du cynisisme léger. In: *Le Monde*, 17. Dezember 1965, S. 12 [Nachruf].

Kochan, Lionel:

Somerset Maugham. In: *The Contemporary Review*, Bd. 177 (Februar 1950), S. 94–98 [*Of Human Bondage*].

Korry, Edward M.:

A Visit with Somerset Maugham. In: *Look*, Bd. 24 (5. Januar 1960), S. 48–50, 53 [Interview].

Somerset Maugham, the World's Richest Writer. In: *Woman's Day*, 7. März 1960.

Krim, Seymour:

Somerset Maugham. In: *Commonweal*, Bd. 61 (3. Dezember 1954), S. 245–250.

Maugham the Artist. In: *Commonweal*, Bd. 61 (10. Dezember 1954), S. 284–287.

Kronenberger, Louis:

The Story-Telling Art of Mr. Maugham. *New York Times Book Review*, 12. August 1934, S. 2 [*East and West*].

Maugham. In: *The Thread of Laughter* (New York, 1952), S. 289–298 [*Our Betters – The Circle*].

Kruschwitz, Hans:

> Die Rassenfrage in W. Somerset Maughams „The Alien Corn". In: *Zeitschrift für Neusprachlichen Unterricht*, Bd. 38 (1939), S. 107–110.

Krutch, Joseph Wood:

> An Epicurean on Liberty. In: *The Nation* (New York), Bd. 153 (4. Oktober 1941), S. 311. Auch in: K.W. Jonas, *The Maugham Enigma*, 1954, S. 205–207 [*Strictly Personal*].

> Machiavellian Philosophy Now and Then. In: *New York Herald Tribune Weekly Book Review*, 2. Juni 1946, S. 1 [*Then and Now*].

> A String of Pearls. In: *The Nation* (New York), Bd. 169 (3. Dezember 1949), S. 549–550 [*A Writer's Notebook*].

Kuner, Mildred C.:

> *The Development of W. Somerset Maugham.* Dissertation, New York University, 1953.

> Maugham and the West. The Human Condition: Bondage. In: K.W. Jonas, *The World of Somerset Maugham*, 1959, S. 37–95.

Kunitz, Stanley J. und Howard Haycraft (Hrsg.):

> Maugham, W.S. In: *Twentieth Century Authors* (New York, 1942), S. 934–936.

Lacretelle, Jacque de:

> La dernière escala de Somerset Maugham. In: *Le Figaro Littéraire*, 23. Dezember 1965, S. 1, 16 [Nachruf].

Lacretelle, Pierre de:

> W. Somerset Maugham, Romancier et Conteur. In: *Gringoire*, 27. November 1931, S. 4 [*Cakes and Ale*].

Land, Myrick:

> The „Ridiculous" Mr. Walpole endures Agonies at the Hands of Mr. Maugham. In: *The Fine Art of Literary Mayhem: A Lively Account of Famous Writers and their Feuds* (New York, 1962), S. 161–179 [*Cakes and Ale – Gin and Bitters*].

Las Vergnas, Raymond:

Le long voyage de Somerset Maugham. In: *Les Nouvelles Littéraires*, 23. Dezember 1965, S. 3 [Nachruf].

Somerset Maugham. In: *La Revue* [*des Deux Mondes*], 15. Januar 1966, S. 171–180.

Lee, Charles:

Mr. Maugham, Still Urbane. In: *New York Times Book Review*, 27. Juli 1947, S. 4, 23 [*Creatures of Circumstance*].

Lehmann, John:

Books and the Arts: A very old Party. In: *New Republic*, Bd. 144 (8. Januar 1966), S. 23–24 [Nachruf].

Lenehan, William T.:

Techniques and Themes in early English and American Naturalistic Novels. Dissertation, University of Oklahoma, 1964 [*Liza of Lambeth*].

Lefèvre, Frédéric:

Une Heure avec W. Somerset Maugham. In: *Les Nouvelles Littéraires*, Jg. 7, Nr. 287 (14. April 1928), S. 1–4.

Lewisohn, Ludwig:

Drama: Somerset Maugham Himself. In: *The Nation* (New York), Bd. 113 (28. September 1921), S. 356. Auch in: K.W. Jonas, *The Maugham Enigma* (1954), S. 104–106 [*The Circle*].

The Case of Somerset Maugham. In: *The Nation* (New York), Bd. 116 (3. Januar 1923), S. 19–20 [*On a Chinese Screen*].

Lindenberger, Raimund:

Autobiographische Konvergenzen in den Kurzgeschichten Somerset Maughams (Passau, 2004).

Littell, Robert:

Outstanding Novels. In:

Yale Review, N.S., Bd. 29 (Winter 1940), S. x [*Christmas Holiday*].
Yale Review, N.S., Bd. 30 (Herbst 1940), S. x. [*The Mixture as Before*].

Yale Review, N.S., Bd. 30 (Sommer 1941), S. xiv [*Up at the Villa*].
Yale Review, N.S., Bd. 32 (Herbst 1942), S. viii. [*The Hour before the Dawn*].

Lockhart, Robert Bruce:

In Kenneth Young's (Hrsg.): *Diaries, 1915–1938* (London, 1973), S. 312–313.

Lurie, Joseph:

W. Somerset Maugham: An Appreciation and a Probe. In: *St. Thomas's Hospital Gazette*, Herbst 1966, S. 112.

Lyons, Leonard:

Maugham-By-the-Sea. In: *Saturday Review*, Bd. 44 (New York, 14. Oktober 1961), S. 44–47, 73–74 [Interview].

MacCarthy, Desmond:

Miscellany: Somerset Maugham. In: *New Statesman*, Bd. 15 (14. August 1920), S. 524–525 [*Caroline – The Unknown*].

Somerset Maugham. The English Maupassant: An Appreciation. In: *Nash's 'Pall Mall' Magazine*, Jg. 91 (Mai 1933), S. 12–15, 66–68 – Sonderdruck (London, 1934), sowie in *Memories* (London, 1953), S. 61–68.

Experience: With the Red Cross 1914–1915 (New York, 1935).

Somerset Maugham. In: *Theatre* (London, 1954), S. 119–139 [Über Maugham als Dramatiker].

W. Somerset Maugham. *The English Maupassant* (New York, 1934).

Makolkin, Anna:

Semiotics of Misogyny through the Humor of Chekhov and Maugham (Lewiston, 1992).

Mander, Raymond und Joe Mitchenson:

Theatrical Companion to Maugham (London, 1955).

The Artist and the Theatre: The Story of the Paintings collected and presented to the National Theatre by W. Somerset Maugham. With an Introduction by W.S. Maugham (London, 1955).

Mann, Dorothea Lawrence:

Somerset Maugham in his Mantle of Mystery. In: *Charles Hanson Towne* (New York, 1925), S. 17–36.

March, Fred T.:

Tales of the East by Somerset Maugham. In: *New York Times Book Review*, 19. November 1933, S. 9 [*Ah King*].

Marchand, Leslie A.:

The Exoticism of Somerset Maugham. In: *Revue Anglo-Américaine*, Jg. 9, Nr. 4 (April 1932), S. 314–328. Auch in: K.W. Jonas, *The Maugham Enigma* (1954), S. 54–71.

Marlow, Louis:

William Somerset Maugham. In: *Seven Friends* (London, 1953), S. 142–170.

Marti-Ibañez, Félix:

Cakes and Manzanilla: The Gentleman from Seville. In: *MD*, Bd. 6 (August 1962), S. 1–14.

Maugham, Frederick Herbert:

Early Days. In: *At the End of the Day* (Westport, 1951).

Maugham, Robin:

My Uncle Willie. In:

Saturday Evening Post, Jg. 239, Nr. 3 (29. Januar 1966), S. 78–81.
Somerset and all the Maughams (London, 1966).
Mein Onkel Somerset und all die Maughams (München, 1967).
Escape from the Shadows. An Autobiography (London, New York, 1972).
Conversations with Willie (New York, 1978).

Maugham, W. Somerset:

Of Human Bondage. With a Digression on the Art of Fiction. In: K.W. Jonas, *The Maugham Enigma* (1954), S. 121–128 [An Address at the Library of Congress on April 20, 1946].

McIver, Claude S.:

William Somerset Maugham: A Study of Technique and Literary Sources. Dissertation, University of Pennsylvania, 1936.

W. Somerset Maugham. In: *Reading and Collection*, Jg. 1 (Juli 1937), S. 5–6, 15.

McKay, L.A.:

Somerset Maugham. In: *Canadian Forum*, Bd. 16 (Mai 1936), S. 23–24 [*Cosmopolitans*].

McKnight, Gerald:

The Scandal of Syrie Maugham (London, 1980).

Mencken, Henry L.:

Point of View. In: *Smart Set Criticism.* (Ithaca, New York, 1968), S. 45–48.

Menard, Wilmon:

The Two Worlds of Somerset Maugham (Los Angeles, 1965) [Einfluß der Französischen Riviera und des Pazifik auf Maughams Werk].

Somerset Maugham in Hollywood. In: *Michigan Quarterly Review*, Bd. 7 (Sommer 1968), S. 207–210.

Middleton, Drew:

Maugham lives a Role he wrote. Author, at 80, becomes cynosure. In: *New York Times*, 26. Januar 1954, S. 25.

Maugham at 90: *The Summing Up*. In: *New York Times*, 25. Januar 1964, S. 20 [Interview].

Always true to Himself. In: *New York Times*, 16. Dezember 1965, S. 50 [Nachruf].

Montague, Clifford M.:

William Somerset Maugham – Dramatist. In: *Poet Lore*, Bd. 47 (Frühjahr 1941), S. 40–55.

Mordaunt, Elinor (Pseudonym: „A. Riposte"):

Gin and Bitters (New York, 1931 / London, 1931, unter dem Titel *Full Circle*).

Morgan, Charles:

Books of the Day: Mr. Maugham's Workshop. In: *Spectator* (London), Bd. 183 (7. Oktober 1949), S. 468. Auch in: K.W. Jonas, *The Maugham Enigma* (1954), S. 208–212 [*A Writer's Notebook*].

Books for Christmas: Maugham's Essays. In: *Spectator* (London), Bd. 189 (12. November 1952), S. 686 [*The Vagrant Mood*].

Morgan, Louise:

Somerset Maugham. In: *Writers at Work* (London, 1931), S. 53–60.

Morgan, Ted:

Maugham (New York, 1980).

Morley, Christopher:

The Maugham Seesaw. In: *New York Times Book Review*, 5. April 1953, S. 5 [*The Vagrant Mood*].

Morris, Alice S.:

Mr. Maugham and the Inquisition. In: *New York Times Book Review*, 7. November 1948, S. 6 [*Catalina*].

Mortimer, Raymond:

Re-reading Mr. Maugham. In: *The New Statesman and Nation*, N.S., Bd. 8 (25. August 1934), S. 243–244 [*Altogether: The Collected Stories* – Britischer Titel: *East and West*].

Current Literature: Books in General. In: *New Statesman and Nation*, N.S., Bd. 19 (23. März 1940), S. 402 [*France at War*].

Books in General: The Fall of France. In: *New Statesman and Nation*, N.S., Bd. 23 (14. März 1942), S. 179–180 [*Strictly Personal*].

Moskovit, Leonard:

Maugham's „*Outstation*": A Single, serious Effect. In: *University of Colorado Studies* [*Series in Language and Literature*] Nr. 10 (Februar 1966), S. 107–114.

Moynihan, Michael:

At the Villa Mauresque. In: *Saturday Times* (London), 12. September 1965.

Muir, Percy H.:

William Somerset Maugham: Some Bibliographical Observations. In: *Book-Collector's Quarterly*, Jg. 9 (Januar bis März 1933), S. 72–84 [Betrifft Frederick T. Bason's Bibliographie (1931)].

Muggeridge, Malcolm:

Somerset Maugham. In: *The Observer*, 19. Dezember 1965, S. 22 [Nachruf].

Natan, Alex:

Somerset Maugham zu seinem 80. Geburtstag. In: *Deutsche Rundschau*, Bd. 80 (Januar 1954), S. 61–65.

Naik, M.K.:

W. Somerset Maugham (Oklahoma University Press, 1966) [*The Moon and Sixpence – Cakes and Ale*].

Naipaul, V.S.:

Liza of Lambeth. In: *Queen's Royal College Chronicle* (Port of Spain, Trinidad), Bd. 23, Nr. 11 (1948), S. 42–43.

Nakano, Yoshio:

Japanese Maugham Studies. An Anthology (Tokio, 1954).

Neuschäffer, Walter:

Dostojewskis Einfluss auf den englischen Roman (Heidelberg, 1935), S. 39–42 [*The Moon and Sixpence*].

Newell, J.P.:

Mr. Somerset Maugham. In: *Times* (London, 24. Dezember 1965), S. 10 [Nachruf].

Nichols, Beverley:
The Twisted Marriage of Somerset Maugham. In: *Look*, Bd. 30 (18. Oktober 1966), S. 33–37 [Auszug aus seinem Band *A Case of Human Bondage* (London, 1966). Betrifft Syrie Maugham und Gerald Haxton, vgl. *Looking Back*].

O' Connor, William Van:

Two Types of Heroes in Post-War Fiction. In: *Publications of the Modern Language Association of America*, Bd. 77 (März 1962), S. 168–174. [J.K. Huysmans – Oscar Wilde – Samuel Butler].

Oku, Yukio:

Some Notes on *Of Human Bondage* (Tokio: University Press, 1952).

Oppel, Horst:

Zwischen Chaos und Erlösung. In: *Die lebenden Fremdsprachen*, Jg. 3 (1951), S. 100–112 [*The Razor's Edge*].

Overton, Grant M.:

The Heterogeneous Magic of Maugham. In: *When Winter comes to Main Street* (New York, 1922), S. 270–285 [Über Maughams Aufenthalt auf Tahiti].

The Somerset Maugham of *The Casuarina Tree*. In: *Bookman* (New York), Bd. 64 (November 1926), S. 298–305.

Papajewski, Helmut:

Die Weltanschauung William Somerset Maughams. In: *Anglia*, Bd. 67–68 (1943/1944), S. 251–317 [Vorabdruck eines Kapitels aus der 1952 erschienenen Monographie].

Die Welt-, Lebens- und Kunstanschauung William Somerset Maughams (Köln, 1952). Vgl. Rolf Soellner.

Paul, David:

Maugham and the Two Myths. In: *Cornhill Magazine*, Bd. 162 (Herbst 1946), S. 143–148. Auch in: K.W. Jonas, *The Maugham Enigma* (1954), S. 156–163 [*The Razor's Edge*].

Pfeiffer, Karl G.:

Maugham – As I know him. In: *Redbook*, Bd. 85 (Mai 1945), S. 40–41, 60–64. Auch in: K.W. Jonas, *The Maugham Enigma* (1954), S. 21–36.

Somerset Maugham, A Candid Portrait. Introduction by Jerome Weidman (New York, 1959).

Pittman, R.N.:

The Maugham Library. In: *The Cantuarian*, Bd. 31, Nr. 4 (Dezember 1966), S. 282–284.

Pollock, John:

Somerset Maugham and his Work. In: *Quarterly Review*, Bd. 304 (Oktober 1966), S. 365–378.

Poore, Charles G.:

Somerset Maugham's Spanish Themes. In: *New York Times Book Review*, 21. Juli 1935, S. 2 [*Don Fernando*].

Books of the Times. In: *New York Times* (2. April 1953), S. 25 [*The Vagrant Mood*].

Books of the Times: The Curtain Speeches of Somerset Maugham. In: *New York Times Book Review*, 5. Oktober 1963, S. 23 [Selected Prefaces and Introductions].

Prescott, Orville:

Outstanding Novels, In: *Yale Review*, Bd. 37 (Herbst 1947), S. 190–191 [*Creatures of Circumstance*].

Books of the Times. In: *New York Times*, 26. Oktober 1948, S. 29. Auch in: K.W. Jonas, *The Maugham Enigm*a (New York, 1954), S. 164–166 [*Catalina*].

Outstanding Novels. In: *Yale Review*, Bd. 38 (Winter 1949), S. 384 [*Catalina*].

Pritchett, V.S.:

Somerset Maugham Revisits Spain. In: *Christian Science Monitor Weekly Magazine Section*, 24. Juli 1935, S. 12 [*Don Fernando*].

Living and Writing. In: *Fortnightly Review*, N.S., Bd. 194 (März 1938), S. 369–370 [*The Summing Up*].

The Mixture as Before. In: *New Statesman and Nation*, N.S., Bd. 19 (15. Juni 1940), S. 750. Auch in: K.W. Jonas, *The Maugham Enigma* (1954), S. 185–190.

Mr. Maugham. In: *New Statesman and Nation*, N.S. Bd. 34 (2. August 1947), S. 94–95 [*Creatures of Circumstance*].

Books in General. *New Statesman and Nation*, Bd. 38 (8. Oktober 1949), S. 401 [*A Writer's Notebook*].

Man of the World. In: *The New Statesman*, Bd. 70, Nr. 1815 (24. Dezember 1965), S. 1008 [Nachruf].

Raphael, Frederic:

Fiction and the Medical Mode. In: *The Listener*, 3. April 1975, S. 452.

Somerset Maugham and his World (New York, 1976).

Rascoe, Burton:

A Chat with Somerset Maugham. In: *A Bookman's Daybook* (New York, 1929), S. 148–153.

Redman, Ben Ray:

In the Days of Machiavelli. In: *Saturday Review of Literature*, Bd. 29 (25. Mai 1946), S. 9–10 [*Then and Now*].

Rees, Leslie:

Remembrance of Things Past: A Meeting with Somerset Maugham. In: *Meanjin Quarterly*, Bd. 26 (Dezember 1967), S. 452–456.

Reyer, Georges:

Le Match de la vie: Le Roman noir d'un héritage. In: *Paris-Match*, Nr. 731 (13. April 1963), S. 6, 10, 14, 19, 26.

Les derniers mots du gentleman du Cap Ferrat: „Je meurs guéri!" In: *Paris-Match*, 25. Dezember 1965, S. 80–81 [Nachruf].

Rhodri, Jeffreys-Jones:

Maugham in Russia. In: *American Espionage: From Secret Service to CIA* (New York, 1977), S. 87–101, 233–235.

Roberts, R. Ellis:

The Art of Somerset Maugham. In: *Saturday Review of Literature*, Bd. 25 (27. Juni 1942), S. 6 [*The Hour before the Dawn*].

Rogal, Samuel J.:

A W. Somerset Maugham Encyclopedia (Westport, Conn., 1997).

Romberg, Bertil:

Studies in the Narrative Technique of the First-Person Novel (Stockholm, 1962), S. 9, 67, 68–69, 77, 78, 330, 331 [Vergleich mit E.T.A. Hoffmanns Technik als angeblicher Herausgeber des Manuskripts eines anderen].

Ross, Woodburn O.:

W. Somerset Maugham: Theme and Variations. In: *College English*, Jg. 8 (Dezember 1946), S. 113–122, auch in *English Journal*, Bd. 36 (Mai 1947), S. 219–228. Auch in: K.W. Jonas, *The Maugham Enigma* (1954), S. 84–100.

Rothschild, Loren, und Deborah Whiteman (Hrsg.):

William Somerset Maugham: A Catalogue of the Loren and Frances Rothschild Collection (Los Angeles, 2001).

Routh, H.V.:

W.S. Maugham. In: *English Literature and Ideas in the Twentieth Century* (London, 1946), S. 5, 146–153, 168.

Salerno, Henry F.:

William Somerset Maugham. In: *English Drama in Transition: 1880–1920* (New York, 1968), S. 463–466 [*Our Betters*].

Sanders, Charles:

W. Somerset Maugham: An Annotated Bibliography of Writings about Him. (Northern Illinois University Press, 1970).

Savini, Gertrud:

Das Weltbild in W. Somerset Maughams Dramen (Erlangen, 1939), Dissertation, Universität Erlangen.

Sawyer, Nevell W.:

W. Somerset Maugham. In: *The Comedy of Manners from Sheridan to Maugham* (Oxford, Philadelphia, 1931).

Schauer Islas, Anita:

William Somerset Maugham (Mexico, 1949). Dissertation, National University of Mexico, 1949 [Spanisch].

Scully, Frank:

Somerset Maugham at Home. In: *Rogue's Gallery: Profiles of My Eminent Contemporaries* (Hollywood, 1943), S. 15–36.

Seidlin, Rosemarie:

Somerset Maugham: *On a Chinese Screen*. In: *Die Neueren Sprachen*, Bd. 13, Nr. 12 (Dezember 1964), S. 573–581.

Shirley, F.J.:

William Somerset Maugham. In: *The Cantuarian* (Canterbury, Dezember 1965), S. 17–18 [Nachruf].

Sitwell, Osbert:

The Spain of Somerset Maugham. In: *London Mercury*, Bd. 32 (September 1935), S. 485–486 [*Don Fernando*].

Obituary of Syrie Maugham. In: *Times* (London), 1. August 1955, S. 9.

Smith, Harrison:

The Imperturbable Mr. Maugham. In: *Saturday Review of Literature*, Bd. 27 (22. April 1944), S. 7–8 [*The Razor's Edge*].

In the great Tradition: Maugham the Master Craftsman. In: *Saturday Review* (New York), Bd. 99 (15. Januar 1966), S. 25 [Nachruf].

Why Maugham was miserable. In: *Books and Bookmen*, Bd. 11 (Februar 1966), S. 22 [Nachruf].

Soellner, Rolf:

> Book Review. In: *Journal of English and Germanic Philology*, Bd. 52 (Oktober 1953), S. 592–594 [Rezension von H. Papajewski, 1952].

Soskin, William:

> A Novelist Ponders Life, Death and God. In: *New York Herald Tribune Books*, 27. März 1938, S. 3 [*The Summing Up*].

Sotheby's Catalogue of the Collection of Impressionist and Modern Pictures formed by W. Somerset Maugham (London, 10. April 1962).

Spencer, Theodore:

> Somerset Maugham. In: *College English*, Bd. 2 (Oktober 1940), S. 1–10. Auch in: K.W. Jonas, *The Maugham Enigma* (1954), S. 72–83 [*Liza of Lambeth – Of Human Bondage – Cakes and Ale – The Summing Up*].

Squire, Sir John:

> Somerset Maugham as Essayist. In: *Illustrated London News*, Bd. 221 (*15. November 1952*), S. 802 [*The Vagrant Mood*].

> Guests at Mr. Somerset Maugham's Party. In: *Illustrated London News*, Bd. 225 (20. November 1954), S. 896 [*Ten Novels and their Authors*].

Standop, Ewald, und Edgar Mertner:

> *Englische Literaturgeschichte* (Heidelberg, 1967) S. 587–588, et al.

Stern, G.B.:

> Somerset Maugham comes of Age. In: *John O' London's Weekly*, Bd. 63 (22. Januar 1954), S. 65–66, 68.

Stokes, Sewell:

> Maugham is Stranger than Fiction. In: *Pilloried!* (New York, 1929), S. 38–53.

> W. Somerset Maugham. In: *Theater Arts*, Jg. 29 (Februar 1945), S. 94–100 [Vgl. mit Checkhov und Shaw].

Stölzel, Thomas und Simone:

Das Normale ist das seltenste Ding auf Erden. Der Menschenkenner und Gentleman-Autor W. Somerset Maugham. In: W. Somerset Maugham: *Notizbuch eines Schriftstellers* (Zürich, 2007), S. 9–85.

Stott, Raymond Toole:

Maughamiana: The Writings of W. Somerset Maugham (London, 1950).

The Writings of William Somerset Maugham: A Bibliography (London, 1956).

A Bibliography of the Writings of W. Somerset Maugham (Edmonten, 1973).

Swan, Michael:

Conversations with Maugham. In: *Ilex and Olive: An Account of a Journey through France and Italy* (London, 1949), S. 67–76.

Swinnerton, Frank:

Somerset Maugham as a Writer. In: *John O' London's Weekly*, Bd. 63 (22. Januar 1954), S. 76–78, Unter dem Titel „Maugham at Eighty" in: *Saturday Review* (New York), Bd. 37 (23. Januar 1954), S. 13–14, 70–72. Auch in: K.W. Jonas, *The World of Somerset Maugham* (London, 1959), S. 12–20.

Maugham and Walpole. In: *Figures in the Foreground: Literary Reminiscences 1917–40* (London, 1963), S. 31–36, 89–94 [*Cakes and Ale* – Hugh Walpole].

Sykes, Gerald:

An Author in Evening Dress. In: *The Nation* (New York), Bd. 133 (25. November 1931), S. 576. Auch in: K.W. Jonas, *The Maugham Enigma* (1954), S. 177–179 [*First Person Singular*].

Taylor, Dwight:

Maugham and the young Idiot. In: *Vogue*, Bd. 122 (1. September 1953), S. 172, 214, 216, 221 [Gerald Haxton].

Taylor, John Russell:

The Rise and Fall of the well-made Play (London, New York, 1967), S. 92–109 et al.

Towne, Charles Hanson (Hrsg.):

> Mr. W. Somerset Maugham at Home. In: *W. Somerset Maugham, Novelist, Essayist, Dramatist* (New York, 1925), S. 8–12.
>
> Vgl. Carl Van Doren, Mark Van Doren, John Farrar, Marcus A. Goodrich und Dorothea L. Mann.

Trilling, Diana:

> Fiction in Review. In: *The Nation* (New York), Bd. 158 (6. Mai 1944), S. 547 [*The Razor's Edge*].

Turner, Helen:

> *Henry Wellcome: The Man, his Collection and his Legacy* (London, 1980).

Vaget, Hans Rudolf:

> Laudatio auf Klaus W. Jonas. In: *Thomas Mann Jahrbuch*, Bd. 11 (1998), S. 109–115.

Van Doren, Carl und Mark:

> W. Somerset Maugham. In: Charles Hanson Towne (New York, 1925), S. 13–16.

Van Doren, Mark:

> Thomas Hardy Veiled. In: *The Nation* (New York), Nr. 131 (29. Oktober 1930), S. 475. Auch in: K.W. Jonas, *The Maugham Enigma* (1954), S. 146–148 [*Cakes and Ale*].

Van Gelder, Robert:

> Mr. Maugham on the Essentials of Writings. *New York Times Book Review*, 24. November 1940, S. 2, auch in *Writers and Writings* (New York, 1946), S. 138–141. Auch in: K.W. Jonas, *The Maugham Enigma* (1954), S. 37–40 [Interview].
>
> Mr. Maugham's Wartime Memoir. In: *New York Times Book Review*, 14. September 1941, S. 9 [*Strictly Personal*].
>
> An Interview with Somerset Maugham. In: *New York Times Book Review*, 21. April 1946, S. 3 [*Of Human Bondage*].

Van Patten, Nathan:

Icelandic Translations of Maugham. In: *Papers of the Bibliographical Society of America*, Bd. 45 (Second Quarter 1951), S. 158–159 – Nachträge zu K.W. Jonas, *More Maughamiana*, Bd. 44 (Oktober 1950), S. 378–390.

Viswanathan, G.V.:

The Novels of Somerset Maugham. In: *Quest (Bombay)*, Nr. 23 (Oktober – November 1959), S. 50–52. [*The Razor's Edge – Of Human Bondage*].

Walpole, Hugh:

William Somerset Maugham: A Pen-Portrait by a Friendly Hand. In: *Vanity Fair: A Cavalcade of the 1920's and 1930's.* (New York, 1960), S. 40–41.

Ward, Richard:

W. Somerset Maugham. An Appreciation (London, 1937).

Wardell, Michael:

A Visit to Somerset Maugham. In: *Atlantic Advocate*, April 1962, S. 26.

Waugh, Alec:

My Brother Evelyn and Other Profiles (New York, London, 1967), S. 272–273.

Waugh, Evelyn:

Books of the Day: The Technician. In: *Spectator* (London), Bd. 162 (17. Februar 1939), S. 274. Auch in: K.W. Jonas, *The Maugham Enigma* (1954), S. 153–155 [*Christmas Holiday*].

Weales, Gerald:

Mr. Maugham on the Novel. In: *Commonweal*, Bd. 62 (27. Mai 1955), S. 212–214 [*An Introduction to Ten Novels and their Authors*].

Religion in Modern English Drama (Philadelphia, 1961), S. 17. 19–21, 279, 280 [*The Unknown*].

Weidman, Jerome:

Introduction. In: *The W. Somerset Maugham Sampler* (Garden City, New York, 1943), S. vii–xxi.

Weightman, John:

Poor Willie. In: *Times Education Supplement* (London), 25. April 1980.

Weintraub, Stanley:

An old Acquaintance. In: *Saturday Review* (New York), Bd. 49 (9. Juli 1966), S. 23–29. [Betrifft Robin Maugham, *Somerset and all the Maughams*].

Wells, James M.:

The Artist in the English Novel, 1850–1919. In: *Philological Studies*, Bd. 4 (September 1943), S. 77–80.

Wescott, Glenway:

Somerset Maugham and Posterity. In: *Harper's Magazine*, Bd. 195 (Oktober 1947), S. 302–31. Auch in: *Images of Truth: Remembrances and Criticism* (New York, 1962), S. 59–85. Sowie in: K.W. Jonas, *The World of Somerset Maugham* (1959), S. 163–179.

West, Rebecca:

W. Somerset Maugham. In: *Nash's Magazine* (Oktober 1935), S. 97.

West, Stanley:

Maugham's Latest. In: *Saturday Review of Literature*, 21. März 1925.

Whitehead, John:

Maugham: A Reappraisal (London, 1987).

Wiebe, Hans:

Die Technik der Kurzgeschichten William Somerset Maughams, Dissertation, Würzburg, 1948.

Williams, Raymond:

The Figure in the Rug. In: *New Statesman*, N.S., Bd. 62 (7. Juli 1961), S. 20–21 [Betrifft Richard A. Cordell's *Somerset Maugham* (1961)].

Wilson, Edmund:

Books: Somerset Maugham and an Antidote. In: *New Yorker*, Bd. 22 (8. Juni 1946), S. 96–99. Auch in: *Classics and Commercials* (New York, 1950), S. 319–326 [*Then and Now*].

Wing, Donald G.:

The Manuscript of Somerset Maugham's *On a Chinese Screen*. In: *Yale University Library Gazette*, Jg. 29 (Januar 1955), S. 126.

Winn, Godfrey:

Maugham: *The Summing Up*. In: *Evening News*, 16. Dezember 1965, S. 4.

The Infirm Glory (London, 1967).

Winterich, John T.:

How this Book came to be. In: *The Moon and Sixpence* (New York, 1941), S. 7–14.

A very old party serves a rich potpourri of Literary Memories. In: *New York Herald Tribune Book Review*, 5. April 1953, S. 5 [*The Vagrant Mood*].

Woods, Katherine:

Somerset Maugham on France at War. In: *New York Times Book Review*, 19. Mai 1940, S. 6.

Zabel, Morton Dauwen:

A Cool Hand. In: *The Nation* (New York), Bd. 152 (3. Mai 1941), S. 534–546, auch in *Craft and Character in Modern Fiction* (New York, 1957), S. 308–312 [*Up at the Villa*].

Zlobina, Maya:

The Surprises of Somerset Maugham. In: *Soviet Review*, Nr. 3 (Juni 1962), S. 3–9 [*The Moon and Sixpence*].

Buchveröffentlichungen von Klaus W. Jonas
Books by Klaus W. Jonas

A Bibliography of the Writings of W. Somerset Maugham. South Hadley, Massachusetts, 1950. XVII, 97 S.

The Maugham Enigma. An Anthology. London: Peter Owen; New York: The Citadel Press, 1954. 217 S.

Carl Van Vechten. A Bibliography. New York: Alfred A. Knopf, 1955. XII, 82 S.

Fifty Years of Thomas Mann Studies. A Bibliography of Criticism. Minneapolis: University of Minnesota Press, 1955. XII, 217 S. Mit einem Vorwort von Thomas Mann: Ein Wort hierzu. – Unveränderte Reprint-Ausgabe: New York: Kraus Reprint, 1969.

The Gentleman from Cap Ferrat. New Haven, Connecticut: Center of Maugham Studies, 1956. 24 S. Mit einem Vorwort von W. Somerset Maugham.

The World of Somerset Maugham. An Anthology. London: Peter Owen; New York: British Book Center, 1959. 200 S. – Unveränderte Reprint-Ausgabe: Westport, Connecticut: Greenwood Press, 1972. 200 S. – Japanische Übersetzung von Mutsuo Tanaka. Tokio: The Hokuseido Press, 1959.

The Life of Crown Prince William. London: Routledge, Kegan Paul, 1961. Amerikanische Ausgabe: Pittsburgh: University of Pittsburgh Press, 1961. 252 S. Englische Übersetzung von Charles W. Bangert.

Der Kronprinz Wilhelm. Frankfurt: Heinrich Scheffler, 1962. 334 S. Vorabdruck: Die Wahrheit über Kronprinz Wilhelm. In: *Welt am Sonntag*, Nr. 11–20 (18. März bis 20. Mai 1962).

Thomas Mann Studies Volume Two. A Bibliography of Criticism. Philadelphia: University of Pennsylvania Press, 1967. 440 S. Autoren: Klaus W. Jonas und Ilsedore B. Jonas (University of Pennsylvania Studies in Germanic Languages and Literature).

Deutsche Weltliteratur von Goethe bis Ingeborg Bachmann (Hrsg.), Festschrift für J. Alan Pfeffer. Tübingen: Max Niemeyer, 1972. XII, 304 S.

Die Thomas-Mann-Literatur. Band I: Bibliographie der Kritik 1896–1955. Berlin: Erich Schmidt, 1972. 458 S. In Zusammenarbeit mit dem Thomas-Mann-Archiv Zürich.

Die Thomas-Mann-Literatur. Band II: Bibliographie der Kritik 1956–1975. Berlin: Erich Schmidt, 1979. 719 S. In Zusammenarbeit mit dem Thomas-Mann-Archiv Zürich.

German and Austrian Contributions to World Literature (1890–1970). Vorwort: D.L. Ashliman. Pittsburgh, Pennsylvania: University of Pittsburgh, 1983. 96 S.

Die Thomas-Mann-Literatur. Band III: Bibliographie der Kritik 1976–1994. Autoren: Klaus W. Jonas und Helmut Koopmann. Frankfurt: Vittorio Klostermann, 1997. XLVII, 614 S. – In Zusammenarbeit mit dem Thomas-Mann-Archiv Zürich.

Fifty Years as a Thomas Mann-Bibliographer – Fünfzig Jahre Thomas Mann-Bibliograph. Mit einem Geleitwort von Thomas Sprecher. Wiesbaden: Harrassowitz Verlag, 2000. XVIII, 157 S.

Zauberberg-Stiftung zur Förderung der Thomas-Mann-Forschung. Autoren: Klaus W. Jonas und Ilsedore B. Jonas. München: Privatdruck, 2002.

Golo Mann. Leben und Werk. Chronik und Bibliographie 1929–2003. Wiesbaden: Harrassowitz Verlag 2003, 343 S. – Zweite verb. und erweit. Auflage, 2004, 366 S. In Zusammenarbeit mit dem Schweizerischen Literaturarchiv Bern. Autoren: Klaus W. Jonas und Holger R. Stunz.

In Vorbereitung: *Die Internationalität der Brüder Heinrich und Thomas Mann. Hundert Jahre Rezeption auf fünf Kontinenten.* Autoren: Klaus W. Jonas und Holger R. Stunz. Frankfurt a. M.: Vittorio Klostermann, 2009.

Index of Personal Names
Personenregister

Adenauer, Konrad 27
Aga Khan 14, 26
Alanson, Bertram 9, 11, 13, 19, 21–23, 25, 66
Amis, Sir Kingsley 24
Auden, Wystan H. 36
Ayer, Alfred 64
Baruch, Bernard 27
Beaton, Sir Cecil 21
Beaverbrook, Lord 21, 40
Beerbohm, Sir Max 31, 45
Behn, Fritz 65, 70
Behrman, S.N. 36
Berenson, Bernard 14
Birkenhead, Lord 62
Burke, Edmund 52
Byron, Lord 41
Chaplin, Charlie 21, 27
Churchill, Sir Winston 15, 21, 27, 53
Clark, Kenneth Lord 21
Congreve, William 31, 45
Connolly, Cyril 36
Conrad, Joseph 30, 42, 48
Cordell, Richard A. 12, 23, 36, 58
Coward, Sir Noël 15, 21, 28, 45
Cronin, Archibald Joseph 39
Cukor, George 16, 28
Day Lewis, Cecil 27
de Gaulle, Charles 27
Defoe, Daniel 41
Dickens, Charles 35
Dietrich, Marlene 27
Dottin, Paul 11, 23, 36, 60
Doubleday, Nelson 12, 13, 22, 24, 25
Doyle, Sir Arthur Conan 39

Dreiser, Theodore 36, 55
Edman, Irwin 13, 25
Elizabeth II, Queen of England 14, 26
Ervine, St. John 32, 36, 62
Fadiman, Clifton 35
Fischer, Kuno 7, 18, 30, 43
Forster, Edward M. 15, 27, 49, 53
Franklin, Benjamin 55
Frederick, Prince of Prussia 64
Gandhi, Mahatma 61
Gauguin, Paul 9, 19, 33, 47, 53
Goebbels, Joseph 32, 55
Goethe, Johann Wolfgang von 52
Gordon, Ruth 16, 21, 28
Greene, Graham 60
Haferkorn, Reinhard 55
Haxton, Gerald 9, 12, 19, 24
Hearn, Lafcadio 48
Heiden, Konrad 12, 23
Heine, Heinrich 41
Hofmannsthal, Hugo von 40
Hope, Lord John 13, 15, 25, 27
Hughes, Ted 24
Jonas, Ilsedore B. 65, 70
Jones, Ethelwyn (Sue) 8, 18
Jones, Henry Arthur 8, 18
Kanin, Garson 21
Kant, Immanuel 52
Kelly, Sir Gerald 8, 18, 21, 66
Kerensky, Alexander 9, 20
King, Francis 63
Kipling, Rudyard 24, 48, 51
Knopf, Alfred A. 70
Köthe, Gottfried 70
Laurencin, Marie 53

Le Carré, John 24
Leidig, Johannes Paul 68
Leon, Fray Luis de 54
Lessing, Doris 24
Lewisohn, Ludwig 36, 60
Loti, Pierre 48
Luce, Claire Booth 16, 28
McEwan, Ian 24
MacCarthy, Sir Desmond 9, 19
Machiavelli, Niccolò 34
Mann, Golo 12, 23
Mann, Heinrich 12, 23, 40
Mann, Thomas 12, 13, 23, 34, 40, 52, 70
Marchand, Leslie A. 50, 60
Marlowe, Christopher 30
Marshall, John 57, 68
Masefield, John 15, 27, 53
Matisse, Henri 53
Maugham, Barbara Sophie (geb. von Scheidlin) 7, 17
Maugham, Edith (geb. Snell) 7, 17
Maugham, Elizabeth (Liza) 9, 11, 13, 19, 21, 22, 25, 28
Maugham, Frederic Herbert, Lord 11, 14, 23, 26
Maugham, Henry MacDonald 7, 17, 30
Maugham, Robert Ormond 7, 17
Maugham, Robert Cecil (Robin), Lord 12, 21, 24
Maugham, Syrie Barnardo Wellcome 9, 10, 14, 19–21, 26
Maupassant, Guy de 33, 47
Morgan, Charles 41, 60
Naipaul, Sir Vidya 24
Nichols, Beverley 21
Nicolson, Sir Harold 36
Niehans, Paul 11, 23, 27, 61, 69
Papajewski, Helmut 36, 55, 59, 68
Paravicini, Vincent 11, 13, 22, 25
Pfeiffer, Karl G. 12, 21, 24, 61, 69
Picasso, Pablo 53
Pius XII., Papst 27
Pritchett, Sir Victor S. 36

Renoir, Pierre-Auguste 53
Rosanoff, Georges 15, 28
Rouault, Georges 53
Sainte-Beuve, Charles Augustin de 33, 47
Schnitzler, Arthur 39, 40
Schopenhauer, Arthur 7, 43
Searle, Alan 10, 12–15, 21, 24, 26–28, 57, 60–65, 69, 70, 72
Shakespeare, William 31, 41
Shaw, George Bernard 31, 40
Sheridan, Richard 31, 45
Shirley, Canon 26
Sisley, Alfred 53
Sitwell, Edith 27
Staley, Thomas F. 69
Stevenson, Robert Louis 48
Sutherland, Graham 25, 53
Swinnerton, Frank 36, 62
Sykes, Gerald 35
Tanaka, Mutsuo 15, 62, 63, 69
Thoma, Ludwig 40
Toscanini, Arturo 63
Trevelyan, George M. 15, 27, 53
Trollope, Anthony 41
Utrillo, Maurice 53
Van Doren, Mark 60
Van Vechten, Carl 22, 69
Walpole, Sir Hugh 30
Wassermann, Jakob 40
Wells, H.G. 22
Werfel, Franz 12, 23, 40
Wescott, Glenway 12, 21, 24, 36, 62
Wheeler, Monroe 21
Wilde Oscar 30, 42, 45
Wilhelm, Kronprinz von Preußen 64, 65, 70
Wilson, Edmund 35
Winn, Godfrey 21
Wycherley, William 31, 45
Zabel, Morton Dauwen 35
Zurbarán, Francisco 25, 52

Index of Places
Ortsregister

Aberdeen 10, 20
Aden 14, 63
Agra 11, 22
Ägypten 8, 10, 14, 18, 21, 26, 53
Angkor Wat 20
Athen 26
Austin, Texas 70
Australien 10, 20, 34, 56
Babylon 35
Bad Gastein 11, 14, 22, 26, 27, 53, 62
Bangkok 53
Bayreuth 53
Beaulieu-sur-mer 21, 65
Belize 10, 21
Benares 11, 22
Berlin 11, 22, 30, 42, 55, 68
Beverly Hills 12, 24
Bombay 11, 14, 22, 63
Borneo 10, 20, 49, 56
Brides-les-Bains 10, 21
British-Honduras 10, 21
Budapest 22
Burma 10, 20, 49
Canterbury, Kent 7, 15, 17, 18, 26, 28, 30, 43, 56
Cap Ferrat 10, 21, 34, 39, 52, 60, 64, 69
Capri 8, 18, 21
Cartagena (Columbia) 22
Ceylon 10, 20, 53
Charles Hill, Farnham (Surrey) 10, 20
Chicago 11, 23
China 10, 20, 2, 47, 49, 56
Cleveland (Ohio) 21
Colombo, Ceylon [Sri Lanka] 10, 14, 20, 63

Columbia 13, 25, 57
Comer See 11, 22
Cuba 10, 21
Cuernavaca 10, 21
Curaçao 22
Deauville 7
Edgartown, Martha's Vineyard, Massachusetts 12, 23
Florenz 8, 11, 14, 18, 23
Frankreich 7, 8, 9, 17, 18, 23, 30, 32, 40, 41, 42, 46, 52, 55, 68
Französisch Guiana 11, 22
Genf 9, 19, 46, 56, 68
Gibraltar 11
Granada 11, 22
Greifswald 55
Griechenland 8, 10, 14, 18, 21, 26, 53, 54
Guatemala 10, 21
Guiana 11
Haiti 11
Hanoi 20
Havana (Cuba) 10, 21
Hawaii 9, 10, 19, 20, 49
Heidelberg 7, 14, 15, 18, 26, 27, 30, 43, 53, 46, 63, 70
Hollywood 34, 52
Hong Kong 14, 63
Honolulu 66
Hyderabad 11, 22
Hyères 17
Indien 11, 13, 22, 25, 34, 48, 49, 56, 58, 61
Indochina 10, 20
Innsbruck 11, 22

128   Index of Places / Ortsregister

Japan 15, 27, 48, 53, 62, 63
Java 56
Jersey City, New Jersey 9, 19, 20, 58
Kalifornien 15, 28, 56, 66
Kobe 14, 63
Köln 68
Kopenhagen 22
Kreta 21
Lafayette, Indiana 12, 23
Lissabon 23
London 8, 9, 11, 12, 16, 18–28, 30, 31, 34, 40, 41, 42, 43, 45, 53, 58, 68, 69
Los Angeles 10, 12, 15, 20, 24, 28, 66
Madras 11, 22
Malaiischer Archipel 49, 56
Mandaley 20
Manila 14, 63
Marokko 25
Marquesas-Inseln 48
Mexico City 10, 21
Mittelamerika 56
Monaco 34
Monte Carlo 15, 28
München 11, 14, 22, 26, 27, 40, 53, 65
New Haven, Connecticut 69
New York 8, 10, 11, 12, 13, 19, 20, 21, 22, 23, 25, 34, 36, 39, 40, 52, 53, 57, 58, 61, 65, 68, 69
Nizza 14, 15, 26, 28, 35
Nordach-on-Dee, Schottland 10, 20
Oxford 14, 26, 53
Panama City 22
Paris 7, 8, 11, 17, 18, 30, 31, 33, 42, 45, 53
Parker's Ferry, Yemassee, South Carolina 12, 24
Pazifik 32, 33
Pau (Pyrenäen) 7
Petrograd 9, 46
Pittsburgh, Pennsylvania 70
Portugal 11, 14, 22, 25
Pressburg/Bratislava 11, 22

Princeton 66
Rapallo 53
Rhodos 10, 21
Rom 9, 19
Saigon 20
Salzburg 11, 21, 22
Samoa 9, 19, 34, 49, 56, 66
San Francisco 10, 11, 13, 19, 20, 22, 23, 25, 66
Schweiz 19, 23, 46, 68
Sea Island (Georgia) 22, 23
Sevilla 11, 22
Siam 10, 20, 49, 56
Singapur 53
Spanien 8, 11, 13, 14, 18, 22, 25, 26, 45, 70
St. Jean, Cap Ferrat 10, 21, 35
St. Laurent du Maroni 11
St. Petersburg/Petrograd 9, 20, 46
Stanford 66, 70
Stockholm 9, 11, 20, 22
Straßburg 23
Südamerika 33, 34, 56
Südsee 46, 47, 49, 53, 55
Tahiti 9, 19, 34, 48, 49, 53, 56
Tarragona 11, 22
Tenafly, New Jersey 9, 19
Tokio 14, 15, 27, 62, 63, 69
Toulouse 11, 23, 53
Türkei 14, 26, 53
Ukraine 30, 42
Valencia 22
Venedig 14, 22, 27, 53, 63
Vevey 11, 23, 61, 69
Vichy 11, 22
Villefranche 65
Washington, D.C. 12, 24, 52
Whitstable, Kent 7, 17
Wien 11, 14, 22, 27, 53, 63
Würzburg 11, 22, 68
Yokohama 63
Yucatan 10, 21
Zürich 57

Index of Works
Werkregister

A Writer's Notebook 12, 24, 29, 34
Ah King 34
Ashenden 9, 19, 32, 46
Cakes and Ale 8, 29, 36, 47
Catalina 13, 34, 52, 68
Catalogue of the Collection of Impressionist and Modern Paintings 34
Ceasar's Wife 32
Creatures of Circumstance 34
Don Fernando 29, 70
For Services Rendered 29, 32
East and West 33
East of Suez 34, 56
France at War 52
Great Novelists and their Novels 30
Liza of Lambeth 8, 18, 31, 32, 45
Looking Back 29, 40
Marriages are made in Heaven 42
Of Human Bondage 13, 24, 25, 32, 42, 46, 55, 74, 75
On a Chinese Screen 29, 34, 56
Purely for my Pleasure 53
Quartet 25
Rain 33, 48
Schiffbrüchig 30, 42
Sheppey 46
Strictly Personal 55, 68
Tellers of Tales 30, 40
The Artistic Temperament of Stephen Carey 13, 25
The Breadwinner 45
The Casuarina Tree 33, 47
The Circle 32
The Constant Wife 32, 45
The Gentleman in the Parlour 29, 34
The Land of the Blessed Virgin 29
The Magician 32, 46
The Moon and Sixpence 29, 32, 46
The Narrow Corner 34
The Painted Veil 32, 47, 56
The Razor's Edge 34, 52
The Sacred Flame 46
The Summing Up 29, 30, 35, 43, 54
The Trembling of a Leaf 33, 47, 66, 92
The Unknown 46
Then and Now 34

About the Illustrations

All possible care has been taken in tracing the ownership of copyright material used in this book and in making acknowledgement for its use. If any owner has not been acknowledged the publishers apologize and will be glad of the opportunity to rectify the error.

Zu den Abbildungen

Der Autor und der Harrassowitz Verlag, Wiesbaden, danken allen Rechteinhabern für die Abdruckgenehmigung. Trotz unserer Bemühungen, alle Inhaber der Rechte festzustellen, ist uns dies in einigen Fällen nicht gelungen. Wir bitten sie deshalb um Entschuldigung und sind gern bereit, diesen Unterlassungsfehler bei nächster Gelegenheit richtigzustellen.

Photographien und Abbildungen wurden bereitgestellt von:
Photographs and Illustrations have been supplied by:

Associated Press, London: 56

Alan Searle, Monaco: 7–14, 21, 22, 24, 48, 49, 59, 61, 65

Carl Van Vechten, Yale University Library: 15–17

Cecil Beaton, London: 60

Doubleday & Co., New York: 41, 42, 44

Edward Quinn Archive, Uerikon: 26–40

Ellinger, Salzburg: 18

Harry Ransom Humanities Research Center Library, The University of Texas at Austin, Austin: 1–6, 46

Ilsedore B. Jonas, München: 51, 52, 63, 66

Islay Lyons, Rom: 43

King's School, Canterbury: 62

Monika Brill, München: 50

Mutsuo Tanaka, Tokio: 53–55

Paul Dottin, Toulouse: 19, 20

Richard A. Cordell, Purdue University, West Lafayette: 23

Ruprecht-Karls-Universität Heidelberg, Heidelberg: 57, 58

Stanford University Libraries, Stanford: 25

The Herbert List Estate, Max Scheler, München: 45

The Tate Gallery, London: Frontispiz

T.S. Strachan, London: 47

Illustrations / Abbildungen

1 Robert Ormond Maugham, the father of WSM
　Robert Ormond Maugham, der Vater von WSM

2 Edith Mary Snell, the mother of WSM
　Edith Mary Snell, die Mutter von WSM

3 Reverend Henry Macdonald Maugham, Vicar of Whitstable, became guardian of WSM upon the death of his Father

Henry Macdonald Maugham, Pfarrer von Whitstable, Adoptivvater von WSM nach dem Tod seines Vaters

4 WSM as a schoolboy
   WSM als Schüler

5 WSM is the third from the left in the front row with his classmates at King's School, Canterbury

WSM als dritter von links in der vordersten Reihe mit seinen Klassenkameraden in der King's School, Canterbury

6 WSM as a student of medicine
WSM als Medizinstudent

7 WSM as a promising young author
   WSM als angehender junger Schriftsteller

8 WSM at the age of twenty-three publishes
   his first novel, Liza of Lambeth
   Mit dreiundzwanzig Jahren schreibt WSM
   seinen ersten Roman, Liza of Lambeth

9 The successful playwright WSM
  Der erfolgreiche Dramatiker WSM

10 WSM shortly after his wedding to Syrie Barnardo
    WSM kurz nach der Eheschließung mit Syrie Barnardo

11 WSM and Syrie Barnardo in the early twenties
    WSM und Syrie Barnardo Anfang der Zwanziger

12 Sue Jones as "Mrs. L. in white", painted by Gerald Kelly
   Sue Jones als „Mrs. L. in white", gemalt von Gerald Kelly

13 Gerald Haxton, WSM's companion and secretary from 1915 until his death in 1944

Gerald Haxton, WSMs Lebenspartner und Sekretär von 1915 bis zu seinem Tod 1944

14 Alan Searle, WSM's friend and companion from 1945 until 1965, in the summer of 1930

Alan Searle, WSMs Freund und Lebenspartner von 1945 bis 1965, im Sommer 1930

15 WSM in London, March 1935
WSM in London, März 1935

16 WSM's favorite snap-shot taken by his friend Carl van Vechten
WSMs Lieblingsbild, aufgenommen von seinem Freund Carl van Vechten

17 WSM and Gerald Haxton
   WSM und Gerald Haxton

18 WSM and Gerald Haxton in Salzburg in the summer of 1935
   WSM und Gerald Haxton im Sommer 1935 in Salzburg

19 WSM awarded an honorary doctorate at Toulouse University by its president, Paul Dottin, 1939

WSM wird 1939 durch den Rektor Paul Dottin zum Ehrendoktor der Universität Toulouse ernannt

20 WSM and Paul Dottin, Toulouse 1939
   WSM und Paul Dottin, Toulouse 1939

21 WSM and his brother Frederick Herbert, the future Lord Maugham, at Bad Gastein in 1936

WSM und sein Bruder Frederick Herbert, der spätere Lord Maugham, in Bad Gastein, 1936

22 Maugham's nephew Robin, after the death of his father Lord Maugham, during a visit with his uncle in the Villa Mauresque

Maughams Neffe Robin, nach dem Tode seines Vaters Lord Maugham, beim Besuch seines Onkels in der Villa Mauresque

23 WSM visits his friend and biographer Richard A. Cordell at Lafayette, Indiana, in 1941

WSM zu Besuch bei seinem Freund und Biographen Richard A. Cordell in Lafayette, Indiana, im Jahr 1941

24 WSM in his study in South Carolina, 1942

WSM in seinem Arbeitszimmer in South Carolina, 1942

25 WSM, his daughter Liza, and his close friends Bertram and Mabel Alanson, during World War II in California

WSM, seine Tochter Liza und die engsten Freunde, das Ehepaar Bertram und Mabel Alanson, während des Zweiten Weltkriegs in Kalifornien

26

27

A visit to the Villa Mauresque. Photographs by Edward Quinn
Zu Besuch in der Villa Mauresque. Photographiert von Edward Quinn

A visit to the Villa Mauresque. Photographs by Edward Quinn
Zu Besuch in der Villa Mauresque. Photographiert von Edward Quinn

30

31

A visit to the Villa Mauresque. Photographs by Edward Quinn
Zu Besuch in der Villa Mauresque. Photographiert von Edward Quinn

A visit to the Villa Mauresque. Photographs by Edward Quinn
Zu Besuch in der Villa Mauresque. Photographiert von Edward Quinn

34

35

A visit to the Villa Mauresque. Photographs by Edward Quinn
Zu Besuch in der Villa Mauresque. Photographiert von Edward Quinn

A visit to the Villa Mauresque. Photographs by Edward Quinn
Zu Besuch in der Villa Mauresque. Photographiert von Edward Quinn

A visit to the Villa Mauresque. Photographs by Edward Quinn
Zu Besuch in der Villa Mauresque. Photographiert von Edward Quinn

A visit to the Villa Mauresque. Photographs by Edward Quinn
Zu Besuch in der Villa Mauresque. Photographiert von Edward Quinn

41 Two passionate bridge players
   Zwei leidenschaftliche
   Bridge-Spieler

42 Never without a cigarette
   Nie ohne Zigarette

43 WSM inscribing a book on Capri, about 1950
   WSM beim Signieren auf Capri, etwa 1950

44 WSM around 1950
    WSM um 1950

45 WSM in 1950
    WSM im Jahre 1950

46 WSM at the opening of an exhibit of the Times Bookshop on January 26, 1954. From left to right: his brother Lord Maugham, his daughter Liza (Lady John Hope) and WSM

WSM bei der Ausstellung des Times Bookshop am 26. Januar 1954. Links sein Bruder, Lord Maugham, in der Mitte Maughams Tochter Liza (Lady John Hope) und WSM

47 WSM and the British actor Eric Portman at the opening of a Maugham Exhibit at the Times Bookshop in London, January 26, 1954

WSM und der britische Schauspieler Eric Portman bei der Eröffnung einer Maugham-Ausstellung des Times Bookshop in London, 26. Januar 1954

48 WSM on his eightieth birthday
   WSM an seinem 80. Geburtstag

49 WSM leaving the Dorchester Hotel in London on his way to a private audience with Queen Elizabeth II in Buckingham Palace, 1954

WSM verlässt das Dorchester Hotel in London vor seiner Auszeichnung im Buckingham Palace durch Königin Elizabeth II, 1954

50 WSM with the sculptor Fritz Behn in Munich

WSM zusammen mit dem Bildhauer Fritz Behn in München

51 WSM in the summer of 1957 in Beaulieu-sur-Mer

WSM im Sommer 1957 in Beaulieu-sur-Mer

52 Alan Searle and Klaus W. Jonas in the summer of 1957 in Beaulieu-sur-Mer

Alan Searle und Klaus W. Jonas im Sommer 1957 in Beaulieu-sur-Mer

53 WSM greeting his admirers on his departure from Tokyo

WSM grüßt zum letzten Mal seine Bewunderer in Japan

54 WSM and Alan in Tokyo

WSM und Alan in Tokio

55 From left to right Alan Searle, Mutsuo Tanaka, sitting next to him on the right WSM
Von links nach rechts Alan Searle, Mutsuo Tanaka, rechts neben ihm sitzend WSM

56 One of his life-long friends, Sir Winston Churchill, on a visit to the Villa Mauresque, about 1958, signed by WSM

Zu Besuch in der Villa Mauresque: der Jugendfreund Sir Winston Churchill, etwa 1958, mit Unterschrift von WSM

57 Heidelberg University: WSM during a discussion with students of the University, May 31, 1961

Universität Heidelberg: WSM während einer Diskussion mit Studenten der Universität, 31. Mai 1961

58 Always willing to answer questions from the public. Heidelberg, May 31, 1961

Immer bereit, Fragen aus dem Publikum zu beantworten. Heidelberg, 31. Mai 1961

59 WSM in conversation
in the drawing-room
of Villa Mauresque

WSM im Gespräch
im Salon der
Villa Mauresque

60 Toward the end of his life WSM
sent copies of this photograph
by his friend Sir Cecil Beaton,
signed both by him and the artist,
to selected friends

Gegen Ende seines Lebens
schickte WSM dieses Bild des
Photographen Sir Cecil Beaton,
von diesem sowie von ihm
unterschrieben, an ausgewählte
Freunde

61 One of the last pictures of WSM together with Alan Searle
   Eines der letzten Bilder von WSM zusammen mit Alan Searle

62 King's School, Canterbury: WSM at the opening of the "Maugham Library" in Canterbury, 1961, donated by WSM

WSM bei der Eröffnung der von ihm gestifteten „Maugham Library" im Jahr 1961

63 Klaus W. Jonas and Peter Henderson, Curator of "The Maugham Library", King's School, September 1999

Klaus W. Jonas und Peter Henderson, Kurator von „The Maugham Library" in der King's School, September 1999

64 Cap Ferrat, from 1928 until the end of his life the permanent home of WSM
Cap Ferrat, von 1928 bis zu seinem Lebensende der ständige Wohnsitz von WSM

65 WSM, Ilsedore B. Jonas and Klaus W. Jonas in the summer of 1960
WSM, Ilsedore B. Jonas und Klaus W. Jonas im Sommer 1960

66 Tombstone of WSM at the wall of Canterbury Cathedral
Grabmal von WSM an der Mauer der Kathedrale von Canterbury